中国 巴中
BAZHONG CHINA

诗意山水 红色巴中

Poetic Landscape and Heroic Bazhong

城市形象标识（LOGO）及巴中旅游形象宣传语
City Image Logo and Tourism Image Slogan of Bazhong

红
叶
知
我
心

巴中欢迎您

巴中文旅康养图志

Bazhong Pictorial Annals on Culture, Tourism and Healthcare

中共巴中市委
巴中市人民政府 编

Compiled by Bazhong Municipal Party Committee and People's Government

方志出版社
Publishing House of Local Records

智勇坚定　排难创新
团结奋斗　不胜不休

Courageous and Determined; Undaunted and Innovative;
United and Hardworking; Ongoing till Victorious

图：剪纸《川陕革命根据地》 李皓迪作品　文：新时代巴中城市精神（红四方面军训词）
Photo: Sichuan-Shaanxi Revolutionary Base (Paper Cutting by Li Haodi)　Text: New-Era Bazhong Spirit (Precept for the Fourth Front Red Army)

川陕苏区首府
秦巴生态名城

Ecologically Famous City in the Qinling and Bashan Mountains and Capital of Sichuan-Shaanxi Soviet Area

巴中城市形象宣传语
City Image Slogan of Bazhong

《巴中文旅康养图志》编纂机构

《巴中文旅康养图志》编委会

顾　问　何　平　高鹏凌　陈建春　李　映　侯中文　喻在岗

主　任　熊文琦　王　毅　任小娟

副主任　赵文峤　陶　斌　温奇志　李洪斌　王祥兵　王永生

委　员　赵建仁　何　渝　李本勇　何金虎　余新颜　郑　琼

张夕谦　陈立平　杨　毅　何小兵　齐小莉　李　旭

王清平　李　骏

《巴中文旅康养图志》编辑部

主　编　李　骏

副主编　蹇黎明　程林斌　王志雄　岳俊峰　杨　婧　杨　娟

编　辑　冉　富　王　胜　杨文佳　周　琳　杨　蝉　罗　娅

朱浩然　毛智慧　徐　武　刘　旭

《巴中文旅康养图志》项目组

组　长　陈　兰　麦　地

成　员　尹雪珊　刘　静　唐晓雅　彭　怡　蒋雯洁　王　可

李晓玲　汪智昊　漆孟涛　高静荣　陈耘莹

《巴中文旅康养图志》翻译组

组　长　曹顺发　康　成

成　员　王兴龙　张　奕

Compiling Team of Bazhong Pictorial Annals on Culture, Tourism and Healthcare

Editorial Board

Consultants	He Ping	Gao Pengling	Chen Jianchun	Li Ying
	Hou Zhongwen	Yu Zaigang		
Directors	Xiong Wenqi	Wang Yi	Ren Xiaojuan	
Deputy Directors	Zhao Wenqiao	Tao Bin	Wen Qizhi	Li Hongbin
	Wang Xiangbing	Wang Yongsheng		
Board Members	Zhao Jianren	He Yu	Li Benyong	He Jinhu
	Yu Xinyan	Zheng Qiong	Zhang Xiqian	Chen Liping
	Yang Yi	He Xiaobin	Qi Xiaoli	Li Xu
	Wang Qingping	Li Jun		

Editorial Department

Editor-in-Chief	Li Jun			
Deputy Editors	Jian Liming	Cheng Linbin	Wang Zhixiong	Yue Junfeng
	Yang Jing	Yang Juan		
Editors	Ran Fu	Wang Sheng	Yang Wenjia	Zhou Lin
	Yang Yang	Luo Ya	Zhu Haoran	Mao Zhihui
	Xu Wu	Liu Xu		

Project Team

Leaders	Chen Lan	Mai Di		
Members	Yin Xueshan	Liu Jing	Tang Xiaoya	Peng Yi
	Jiang Wenjie	Wang Ke	Li Xiaoling	Wang Zhihao
	Qi Mengtao	Gao Jingrong	Chen Yunying	

Translation Team

Leaders	Cao Shunfa	Kang Cheng
Members	Wang Xinglong	Zhang Yi

巴中文旅康养示意图

A Sketch Map of Culture, Tourism and Healthcare in Bazhong

本示意图为手绘图　非准确地理地图

A Hand-Drawn Map Only

前言

美丽中国　青春山河

北望秦川八百里，俯瞰巴蜀万重山。地处华夏版图腹心地带，被誉为“南方的北方，北方的南方”，这里是巴中。

巴人南征北战，巴国与群雄争锋，巴文化归流华夏文明，历史光芒和缥渺身姿同样让人痴迷和向往，这就是巴中。

川陕忠魂，光耀千秋，由此创建全国第二大苏区，红军精神、红色旅游与天赐诗意山水相映成辉，这也是巴中。

伴随着光雾山与诺水河声名远播、全域旅游战略的渐次推进，文旅康养首位产业发展愈发坚定铿锵，这才是巴中。

巴中之美，在于山水之奇，在于人文之盛，在于物产之丰，在于山河日新，在于为美丽中国贡献了靓丽样板、生动实践。

与秦岭并行的巴山巴岭是中国山河最写意的存在，它挡住了西北风的长驱直入、直下江南，在北纬 31 °区域造就了罕见的多样性生物基因库和人类文化舒适带。光雾山魔幻般的小环境四时景色万象新，亚洲最长红地毯为“万山红遍，层林尽染”提供了最佳实景；诺水河与光雾山同为世界地质公园，举世罕见的地下溶洞群是上天为满足人们的好奇心、猎奇感、求知欲而专门以鬼斧神工的手法设置的别有洞天。空山、神门、临江，随处都可见造物神奇和上苍之眷顾，巴中有幸。

从可考的新石器时代开始，巴子国地就习惯性创造着属于自己的传奇，让世艳羡，令人向往。《华阳国志》的记述，第一次让巴人以主人公身份登上历史舞台，由此以降，米仓凿道、蔓子义楚、刘邦得汉、萧何截贤、章怀望王、思邈洗药、商隐遇雨、八柱抗元、湖广填川，历朝历代，巴中风流可圈可点，巴中人物尽心尽力。近现代以来，红四方面军创建的川陕革命根据地为苏维埃架起了南北桥梁、为新中国做出了重大牺牲，为后来者树立了光辉典范。追思及近，晏阳初带着执着的乡情奉献世界，吴伟仁为大国重器增添华彩，油画《父亲》贡献一个时代的人文原版，人杰地灵，巴中有福。

大好河山重安排，奋发有为定胜天，老区人民正以崭新的青春姿态，自信地迎接中国式现代化，为传统人文、诗意山水、红色文化赋予新的内涵、新的价值。星罗棋布的传统村落可以让隐居乡里不再是奢望，风格各异的现代新居可以让自在慢生活触手可及，古风湛然的农耕文化可以让风雨有温度有味道，而这一切看得见的乡愁与现代都市仅仅一墙之隔、一米之遥。旅游并不是简单的来来往往，快慢之间的转换切换本身就是人生境界的跃升，修身、修心、修性、修道的多重功效叠加让巴中康养更有灵魂、更有归属感。诗意栖居，巴中有礼。

一图览一域，满纸尽芳菲。送您诗意山水，相逢红色巴中，巴中有您更精彩、更美丽、更青春，让本图志成为我们之间的信使吧！

编者

2022 年 12 月

Preface

Bazhong Landscape, Part of Beautiful China

From an aerial view of the Qinling Mountains of eight hundred miles and the numerous mountains in the Bashu region (present-day Sichuan and Chongqing), one can easily place the area called Bazhong, located in the heart of China's territory and known as its "north of the south and south of the north".

The Ba people fought south and north as their kingdom vied with the others, yet Ba culture has always stayed part of the Chinese civilization. Bazhong, owing to its brilliant history and ethereal status, still enchants those who yearn for it.

The loyal souls of Sichuan and Shaanxi remain immortal forever, owing to their establishment in China of the second largest Soviet area. The Red Army spirit, red tourism and poetic landscape bestowed by Nature complement each other. This is also Bazhong.

With the reputation of Nuoshui River in Mt. Guangwu and the gradual advancement of global tourism strategy, its top-priority development of culture, tourism and Healthcare has become increasingly healthy and sturdy. This is Bazhong in its true sense.

The beauty of Bazhong lies in the wonders of its mountains and rivers, in the prosperity of its cultural richness, in the abundance of its products, in the daily innovation of its social progress, and in the contribution of beautiful models and vivid practices to a beautiful China.

The Bashan Mountains, running alongside those of Qinling, are the most poetic existence in China, the reason being that they have blocked the long and direct thrust of the northwest wind toward the Yangtze River and created a rare diversity of biological gene pools and human cultural comfort zones in the area of 31 degrees north latitude. The magical small environment of Mt. Guangwu is full of new scenery in all seasons, and makes the best real scene of the longest red carpet in Asia owing to its "red-dyed mountains". Both Nuoshui River and Mt. Guangwu are world geoparks, where the rare underground karst caves are uniquely cut by heaven to satisfy human curiosity, hunt and thirst for knowledge. It is lucky of Bazhong to see everywhere in Kongshan, Shenmen, and Linjiang such magic creations and heavenly blessings.

Since the examinable Neolithic Age, the Kingdom of Ba has habitually created its own legend, to the envy and admiration of the rest world. By the record of *Huayang Guozhi*, the Ba people appeared on the stage of history for the first time. From then on, those who hewed out the Micang Ancient Road, General Manzi who sacrificed himself for his kingdom, Liu Bang who founded the Han Dynasty, Xiao He who recommended talent, Prince Zhanghuai who got a wrongful death, Sun Simiao who washed herbs, Li Shangyin who met with nightly rains, the eight battlefield sites against the Yuan invaders, and innumerable people in the Qing Dynasty who relocated to Sichuan—all this shows what Bazhong has selflessly dedicated. Since modern times, the Sichuan-Shaanxi Revolutionary Base established by the Fourth Front Red Army has built a north-south bridge for the Soviets, made great sacrifices for the founding of New China in 1949, and set a shining example for the latecomers. Reminiscing about the near past, we cherish the memory of Yan Yangchu who dedicated himself to the world with his persistent nostalgia, Wu Weiren who added splendor to China as a major country, and the oil painting of *Father* that contributed to the contemporary cultural original. All these are a sign of outstanding people in the blessed place of Bazhong.

Thanks to the great era when all the Chinese people are striving for a better life, those in this old revolutionary area are confidently marching on the new Chinese path to modernization with a new youthful attitude, and enriching traditional culture, poetic landscape, and revolutionary culture with new connotations and new values. The dotted traditional villages can make living in seclusion no longer a luxury. The modern new residences with different styles can bring a comfortable and slow life within easy reach. The ancient farming culture can make the wind and rain warm and tasteful. It is only one wall and one meter away that all these visible nostalgia from the modern city. Traveling is not simply coming and going. The switching between fastness and slowness is itself a leap in the realm of life. The superposition of multiple effects of physical and mental cultivation, and monasticism gives Bazhong's Healthcare more soul and a greater sense of belonging. Poetic living has been turning Bazhong all the more polished.

Each photo shows a scene while every page is full of beauty. Welcome to Bazhong to enjoy its poetic landscape and bathe in its revolutionary atmosphere. It will be more exciting, more beautiful, and more youthful because of your arrival. May this book serve as a messenger between us!

Editorial board
December 2022

凡例

一、《巴中文旅康养图志》以马克思列宁主义、毛泽东思想、邓小平理论、“三个代表”重要思想、科学发展观、习近平新时代中国特色社会主义思想为指导，坚持辩证唯物主义和历史唯物主义的立场、观点和方法，全面、客观地记述巴中文化、旅游、康养发展的历史与现状，力求思想性、资料性、科学性相统一。

二、本图志上限为民国 17 年（1928），下限至 2022 年，以 1993—2022 年为主要记述时段，为保持事项的完整性，个别事项适当上延。

三、本图志采用篇、章结构，共三篇、十章，每一章下设综述，综合记述该章内容及部分知识点。

四、本图志以图片和照片（以下简称“图照”）为主要记述内容，图注文字包括图照所反映的主要内容、拍摄者或供图者等信息。

五、本图志中文部分记述使用规范的现代语体文，行文力求严谨、朴实、简洁、流畅。

六、本图志文字资料主要来源于公开出版或内部出版的市、县（区）志书、专业志、年鉴、大事记，以及向相关单位采编的资料，文内不标注出处。图照主要来源为向相关组织购买，以及相关部门个人提供，在图照文字中标明了拍摄者或供图者。

七、本图志使用规范汉字，数字用法、计量单位、标点符号分别执行国家标准《出版物上数字用法》（GB/T 15835—2011）、《中华人民共和国法定计量单位》和《标点符号用法》（GB/T 15834—2011）。

Explanatory Notes

1. Guided by Marxism-Leninism, Mao Zedong Thought, Deng Xiaoping Theory, the important thought of "Three Represents", the Scientific Outlook on Development, and Xi Jinping Thought on Socialism with Chinese Characteristics for a New Era, *Bazhong Pictorial Annals on Culture, Tourism and Healthcare* sticks to the position, viewpoint and method of historical materialism when comprehensively and objectively describing the history and status quo of Bazhong's development of culture, tourism and healthcare, and strives for an ideological, referential and scientific unity;

2. This book starts from the 17th year of the Republic of China (1928) to the end of 2022, with 1993-2021 as the main period. For its completeness, some individual items are appropriately extended;

3. It adopts the structure of parts and chapters, which totals three and ten, respectively. Each chapter has a summary, which comprehensively describes its content and some knowledge points as well;

4. It is mainly composed of pictures and photos (hereinafter referred to as photos), including such information as their main content and photographers;

5. The Chinese text of this book, as required by standard modern Chinese, is rigorous, simple, concise and fluent;

6. The written materials of this Pictorial Annals are mostly taken from the publicly or internally published city, county (district) record, professional record, yearbook and chronicle of events, and the materials collected and compiled by relevant units, so the source is not included in the text. The main sources of photos are either purchased from the organizations or provided by individuals concerned, and their names are shown right after;

7. The use of standard Chinese characters in this book, and of numbers, units of measure, and punctuation marks in conformity with the national standards for the General Rules for Writing Numerus in Public Texts (GB/T 15835-2011), Legal Unit of Measurement of PRC and General Rules for Punctuation (GB/T 15834-2011).

目录
CONTENTS

巴中市文旅集团供图
燕岭仙岛景点

Photo / Courtesy of Bazhong Cultural Tourism Group
Yanling Fairyland

大事记

1928 年

巴中巴河南岸的回风亭竣工落成。

1932 年

12 月，红四方面军从通江两河口进入四川。

1933 年

年初，红四方面军将通江县城诺江公园扩展更名为列宁公园。

2 月，中共川陕省委宣传部在通江县城壁山悬崖錾刻“争取苏维埃中国”石刻标语。此为川陕革命根据地内第一幅石刻标语。

7 月，巴中特别市委、巴中特别市苏维埃成立。

1934 年

3 月，红四方面军总政治部錾字队在通江县沙溪嘴景家塬高崖錾刻巨幅标语“赤化全川”。红四方面军錾字队在通江县至诚九子坡佛耳岩錾刻巨幅标语“平分土地”。

10 月，通江县王坪红军烈士墓建成。

1951 年

巴中县建县人民文化博物馆。

1958 年

巴中县革命博物馆建成。

1961 年

巴中县革命博物馆更名为川陕革命根据地巴中纪念馆。

1976 年

在巴中县酒店乡（巴中市恩阳区渔溪镇）发现月亮岩遗址，为新石器时代聚落遗址。

在南江县发现断渠遗址，为新石器时代遗址。

1977 年

在南江县发现阳八台遗址，为新石器时代遗址。

1979 年

3 月，川陕革命根据地巴中纪念馆更名为川陕革命根据地博物馆。

1982 年

12 月，通江县将县城文庙辟为川陕革命根据地军史陈列馆。

1984 年

在通江县春在乡发现擂鼓寨遗址，为新石器时代遗址。

1985 年

通江县王坪红军烈士墓更名为王坪烈士陵园。

1986 年

7 月，通江县诺水河景区正式对外开放。

10 月，刘伯坚烈士纪念馆（碑）落成。

1988 年

1 月，巴中南龛摩崖造像、红四方面军总指挥部旧址、红四方面军总政治部旧址、红四方面军王坪烈士墓及墓碑被公布为“全国重点文物保护单位”。

1989 年

8 月，王坪烈士陵园被批准为“全国烈士纪念性建筑物重点保护单位”，被命名为“全国爱国主义教育示范基地”。

1991 年

1 月，巴州城、通江城被命名为“四川省历史文化名城”。

7 月，通江县将王坪烈士陵园更名为红四方面军王坪烈士陵园。

9 月，通江县举办首届通江银耳节。

是年，巴中县建成晏阳初博士史迹展览馆。

1992 年

10 月，川陕革命根据地军史陈列馆更名为红四方面军总指挥部旧址纪念馆。

是年，恩阳古镇被命名为“四川省历史文化名镇”。

1993 年

7 月，国务院批准成立巴中地区。

9 月，四川省人民政府批准在巴中南龛公园建立川陕苏区将帅碑林。

12 月，南江县光雾山风景区被批准为省级风景名胜区。

1995 年

4 月，通江县被命名为“中国银耳之乡”。

5 月，诺水河—光雾山风景名胜区被列入全省开发和改造十大旅游项目之一。

1998 年

9 月，中国地质学会洞穴研究会会长、地质学家朱学稳对通江县诺水河风景区实地考察。他指出，诺水河风景区是名副其实的喀斯特之乡和溶洞之乡。

2000 年

9 月，川陕革命根据地博物馆被命名为“全国青少年教育基地”。

12 月，撤销巴中地区，成立巴中市。

2001 年

3 月，巴中南龛、北龛、西龛、水宁寺摩崖造像被公布为“全国重点文物保护单位”。

是月，中共中央政治局常委、书记处书记、国务院副总理温家宝到巴中调研指导。

6 月，红四方面军总指挥部旧址纪念馆被命名为“全国爱国主义教育示范基地”。

12 月，中国洞穴协会会长朱学稳到通江县诺水河中峰洞考察，指出中峰洞堪称“天下第一洞”

2002 年

4 月，首届“四川 · 巴中 2002 巴人文化艺术节”在巴城江北白云台开幕。

8 月，红四方面军王坪烈士陵园更名为川陕革命根据地红军烈士陵园。

10 月，川陕片区旅游协作会在南江县桃园镇举行。

是月，南江县举办 2002 · 光雾山红叶节。

12 月，南江县米仓山森林公园被批准为“国家森林公园”。

2003 年

10 月，首届中国 · 四川光雾山红叶节在南江县桃园开幕。

12 月，平昌镇龙山被批准为“国家森林公园”。

是年，巴山游击队纪念馆扩建。

2004 年

1 月，光雾山 · 诺水河被批准为“国家重点风景名胜区”。

9 月，四川 · 通江溶洞之乡银耳节在通江县开幕。

12 月，巴中市巴州区天马山、通江空山被批准为“国家森林公园”。

是年，巴中被列为全国“重点红色旅游区”中的“川陕渝红色旅游区”、全国 30 条“红色旅游精品线路”、全国 100 个“红色旅游经典景区”。

2005 年

4 月，中共中央政治局常委、国务院总理温家宝到巴中调研指导。

7 月，川陕苏区将帅碑林纪念馆落成。

10 月，第一届巴中旅游发展大会在南江县光雾山镇召开。

是月，巴中市巴州区恩阳镇被命名为“全国文明村镇”。

11 月，川陕苏区将帅碑林被命名为“全国爱国主义教育示范基地”。

是月，平昌县被评为“全国文化先进县”。

2006 年

6 月，通江千佛岩石窟、通江红军石刻标语群被公布为“全国重点文物保护单位”。

是月，巴山背二歌被列入国家级非物质文化遗产名录。

10 月，第一届中国 · 四川南江黄羊节在南江县开幕。

2007 年

8 月，南江县被评为“中国生态旅游大县”。

9 月，南江县被命名为“中国红叶之乡”。

是年，巴山游击队纪念馆被命名为“四川省爱国主义教育基地”。

2008 年

1 月，中共中央政治局常委、国务院副总理李克强到巴中调研指导。

4 月，巴中市被列入全省红色旅游重点发展的 3 大红色旅游主题之一的川陕苏区主题，6 个红色旅游重点片区之一的川陕革命根据地旅游片区，8 条精品红色旅游线路之一的川陕苏区精品旅游线。

6 月，翻山铰子被列入国家级非物质文化遗产名录。

9 月，平昌县江口水乡水利风景区被批准为“国家水利风景区”。

10 月，南江县被命名为“中国富硒茶之乡”。

12 月，巴中市巴州区恩阳镇被命名为“中国历史文化名镇”。

是年，巴中市巴州区曾口镇被命名为“中国民间文化艺术之乡”。

是年，南江县光雾山镇被命名为“全国文明村镇”。

2009 年

4 月，光雾山红叶节被列为全国主要节庆活动。

是月，川陕甘渝“三国文化旅游精品线路”启动仪式上，联合推出三国文化旅游精品线路，巴中被列入大三国旅游环线。

2010 年

2 月，光雾山旅游景区被批准为国家 AAAA 级旅游景区。

是月，通江县空山乡被评为省“生态旅游百佳乡”。

2011 年

7 月，红四方面军总指挥部旧址纪念馆被命名为“全省首批廉政教育基地”。

12月，巴中市巴州区柳林镇玉金村等2个村被命名为“全国文明村镇”。

2012年

2月，通江县诺江镇、平昌县驷马镇、南江县长赤镇被评为“省级生态乡镇”。

3月，巴山游击队纪念馆开馆。

是月，四川省文物考古研究院组织国家博物馆等15家单位，开展为期13天的“米仓古道”考古探险调查活动。

5月，中国工农红军第四方面军总医院旧址群被命名为“全国卫生系统爱国主义教育基地”。

12月，米仓古道入选《中国世界文化遗产预备名单》。

2013年

1月，平昌县被命名为“全国休闲农业与乡村旅游示范县”“四川省乡村旅游示范县”。

2月，通江王坪旅游景区、南江米仓山旅游景区被批准为国家AAAA级旅游景区。

3月，四川巴中·平昌首届乡村旅游文化节在平昌县开幕。

4—5月，南江县先后被命名为“中国最佳养生休闲旅游名县”“中国休闲度假养生养老福地”。

6月，巴城望王山运动公园正式开园，该园是巴中市首个集生态保护、休闲娱乐、运动健身、观光于一体的城市生态运动主题公园。

2014年

2月，平昌县白衣镇被命名为“中国历史文化名镇”。

4月，四川省第五届乡村文化旅游节在平昌县举行。

5月，诺水河旅游景区、佛头山旅游景区被批准为国家AAAA级旅游景区。

6月，巴中市被命名为“四川省园林城市”。

是月，巴中市恩阳镇、光雾山镇、沙河镇、白衣镇、诺水河镇被命名为“国家级生态乡镇”。

7月，巴中市被命名为“全省旅游标准化示范市”，平昌县、通江县被命名为“全省旅游标准化示范县”。

9月，通江县沙溪镇王坪村被命名为“全国生态文化村”。

12月，平昌县被命名为“中国民间文化艺术之乡”。

12月，光雾山景区被批准为“省级旅游度假区”

2015年

1月，巴中化湖水利风景区被批准为“国家水利风景区”。

2月，平昌县巴灵台旅游景区被批准为国家AAAA级旅游景区。

是月，巴中市巴州区清江镇巾字村等2个村被命名为“全国文明村镇”。

4月，首届“巴中云顶”茶文化旅游节在南江县元顶子村云顶广场举行。

6月，巴中市被命名为“中国石刻艺术之乡”。

7月，巴中市米仓山、空山、镇龙山、天马山国家森林公园被评为全省10大“最佳森林康养目的地”。

8月，平昌县首届茶文化旅游节在鹿鸣镇石龙村举行。

12月，南江县红光镇玉白村被命名为“全国生态文化村”。

是月，南江县醉美玉湖·七彩长滩旅游景区、平昌县驷马水乡旅游景区被批准为国家AAAA级旅游景区。

2016年

2月，平昌县入选首批“四川省乡村旅游强县”。

7月，巴中市巴州区被命名为“中国曲艺之乡”。

10月，巴中市巴州区南龛山旅游景区、巴中市巴州区山水化湖旅游景区、巴中市恩阳区恩阳古镇、通江县空山天盆旅游景区、南江县云顶茶乡旅游景区被批准为国家AAAA级旅游景区。

11月，巴中市被命名为“全国生态文明城市”，光雾山景区被评为“全国生态文明景区”。

是月，巴中市巴州区光辉镇白鹤山村等10个村被列入中国传统村落名录。

是年，平昌县被评为“全国十佳宜居县”。

2017年

1月，米仓山国家森林公园等4个国家森林公园被命名为“四川省首批国家级森林氧吧”。

3月，通江县唱歌石林森林康养基地等2个森林康养基地被命名为“四川省森林康养基地”。

5月，全省森林康养产业发展推进会在南江县召开。

7月，巴中市被命名为“国家卫生城市”。

8月，南江县玉湖被批准为“国家水利风景区”。

9月，南江米仓山国家森林公园、通江唱歌乡石林景区入选“全国森林康养基地试点单位”。

10月，巴中市被命名为“国家森林城市”。

11月，米仓山森林康养基地被命名为四川首批“森林康养国际合作示范基地”。

是月，通江县空山乡中坝村等4个村被命名为“全国文明村镇”。

12月，《巴中市红军文物保护条例》经省人大常委会批准实施。

是月，巴中市委四届五次全会提出大力发展生态旅游、森林康养，加快建成全国知名旅游目的地和森林康养目的地，打造旅游经济强市。

是月，巴中市恩阳区章怀山森林康养基地等5个森林康养基地被命名为“四川省森林康养基地”。

是年，平昌县云台镇龙尾村被命名为“中国美丽休闲乡村”。

2018年

3月，平昌县白衣古镇旅游景区和皇家山旅游景区被批准为国家AAAA级旅游景区。

4月，南江县光雾山镇、通江县空山镇被命名为“全国最美森林小镇”。

是月，光雾山—诺水河地质公园获联合国教科文世界地质公园。

10月，通江县壁山森林康养基地等8个森林康养基地被命名为“四川省森林康养基地”。

是月，平昌县鹿鸣镇石龙村被命名为“中国美丽休闲乡村”。

11月，巴中获评“2018年度《中国国家旅游》最佳全域旅游目的地”。

12月，《巴中市石窟保护条例》获省人大常委会批准实施，是四川省第一部石窟文物保护领域的地方性法规。

是月，巴中市恩阳区兴隆镇玉皇村等14个村被列入中国传统村落名录。

是月，巴中市恩阳区获全国“绿水青山就是金山银山”实践创新基地。

是月，南江县被命名为“国家生态文明建设示范县”。

是月，巴中柳津湖水利风景区被批准为“国家水利风景区”。

是月，通江县毛浴镇被命名为“中国历史文化名镇”。

是年，巴中市巴州区七彩佛龛景区、巴中市恩阳区万寿养生谷旅游景区被批准为国家AAAA级旅游景区。

2019年

2月，巴中市巴州区天马山国家森林公园被命名为“中国森林养生基地”。

是月，平昌县龙岗镇、南江县杨坝镇被命名为“中国民间文化艺术之乡”。

6月，巴中市5条红色旅游线路入选全省红色旅游推荐线路。

8月，巴中川陕苏区主题线路被列入全省第二批红色旅游线路。

是月，全国首部行浸式山水夜游旅游剧目《梦境光雾山》与游客正式见面。

10月，通江县泥溪镇犁园坝村等4个村被评为“四川最美古村落”。

是月，石门寺石窟被公布为“全国重点文物保护单位”。

11月，通江县唱歌石林旅游景区被批准为国家AAAA级旅游景区。

2020年

5月，光雾山—诺水河世界地质公园与达古冰山国家地质公园缔结为“姊妹公园”。

6月，南江县米仓山森林康养基地被命名为“国家森林康养基地”。

是月，巴中市恩阳区下八庙镇万寿村等4个村被命名为“四川省首批乡村旅游重点村”。

7月，四川省第十一届（夏季）乡村文化旅游节在南江县光雾山铁炉坝广场开幕

9月，南江县被命名为“天府旅游名县”。

是月，四川省向人民英雄敬献花篮仪式在川陕革命根据地红军烈士陵园举行。

是月，南江县赤溪镇西厢村被命名为“中国美丽休闲乡村”。

10月，平昌县获全国“绿水青山就是金山银山”实践创新基地。

是月，巴中市被命名为“中国气候养生之都”。

11月，南江县光雾和谷森林康养基地等3个森林康养基地入选“全国森林康养基地试点建设单位”。

是月，恩阳古镇当选“巴蜀文化旅游走廊新地标”。

是月，通江县沙溪镇王坪村等5个村被命名为“全国文明村镇”。

12月，巴中市被确定为“全国旅游标准化示范单位”。

是月，巴中市光雾山景区被批准为国家AAAAA级旅游景区。

是月，平昌驷马河湿地公园被批准为“平昌驷马河国家湿地公园”。

2021年

1月，巴中经开区九寨山景区、平昌县大石童话景区被批准为国家AAAA级旅游景区。

4月，大型情境式夜游剧目《恩阳船说》开演。

6月，红四方面军总指挥部旧址纪念馆等6个红色景区景点被列入“建党百年红色旅游百条精品线路”之“奇兵入川·铁血丹心”精品线路。

7月，巴中恩阳机场北京大兴—巴中等3条航线入选首批国家红色旅游精品航线。

是月，川陕革命根据地红军烈士陵园被命名为“全国妇女爱国主义教育基地”。

9月，巴中市发布城市形象标识（LOGO）和市树市花。

是月，通江县沙溪镇王坪村被命名为“天府旅游名村”。

10月，通江县被命名为“国家生态文明建设示范县”。

11月，巴中市光雾山诺水河文旅融合发展示范区在南江县光雾山镇挂牌成立。

是月，巴中市首届文旅康养发展大会在南江县召开。

是月，南江县被命名为“四川省全域旅游示范区”。

是月，巴中市第五次党代会提出要突破发展文旅康养首位产业，实施文旅强市战略。

12月，巴中市被评为“全国最美生态宜居典范城市”。

是月，“诗意山水，红色巴中”宣传片正式登陆央视新闻频道，开启巴中文旅品牌传播新格局。

是月，第七届光雾山冰雪节开幕。

2022年

1月，全国首条红色主题高速公路—镇（巴）至广（安）高速王（坪）至通（江）段正式通车。

3月，“田园恩阳·海山情园”首届油菜花节在柳林现代农业产业园开幕。

6月，首届四川诺水河国际溶洞节在通江县诺水洞天景区开幕。

7月，第十届巴人文化艺术节在巴中市体育馆开幕。

是月，第七届“巴中云顶”茶文化旅游节在南江县开幕。

是月，巴中市文旅新区光雾山镇被命名为“天府旅游名镇”，南江县西厢村被命名为“天府旅游名村”。

8月，“划遍四川”2022年恩阳龙舟公开赛在恩阳龙舟公园开幕。

11月，通江县被命名为“天府旅游名县”。

是月，第二十届四川光雾山国际红叶节在巴中市文旅新区光雾山镇铁炉坝广场开幕。

是月，巴中市恩阳区下八庙镇万寿村被命名为“中国美丽休闲乡村”。

是月，巴中市被命名为“国家生态文明建设示范区”。

12月，巴中市巴州区、巴中市恩阳区、平昌县被命名为“四川省全域旅游示范区”。

Chronicle of Events

1928

Huifeng Pavilion on the south bank of Bahe River, Bazhong, was completed.

1932

In December, the Fourth Front Red Army entered Sichuan from Tongjiang's Lianghekou.

1933

Early the year, the Fourth Front Red Army enlarged Tongjiang's Nuojiang Park and renamed it Lenin Park.

In February, the Publicity Department of Sichuan-Shaanxi Provincial Committee of CPC had the slogan "Strive for Soviet China" carved on the cliff of Tongjiang's Mt. Chengbi, the first ever stone slogan in Sichuan-Shaanxi Revolutionary Base.

In July,Bazhong Special Municipal Party Committee and Soviet Government was established.

1934

In March, the chisel team of the General Political Department of the Fourth Front Red Army carved huge slogans "A Revolutionary Sichuan" on the high cliff of Jingjiayuan, Shaxizui, and "Equal Distribution of Land" on Fo'er Crag in Tongjiang's Jiuzipo, Zhicheng Town.

In October, Wangping Tomb of Red Army Martyrs in Tongjiang was completed.

1951

Bazhong County People's Cultural Museum was built.

1958

Bazhong County's Revolutionary Museum was built.

1961

Bazhong County's Revolutionary Museum was renamed as Bazhong Memorial Hall of Sichuan-Shaanxi Revolutionary Base.

1976

The Moon Rock Site, discovered in Jiudian Township, Bazhong County (present-day Yuxi Town, Enyang District, Bazhong), is a Neolithic settlement one.

The Broken Canal Site, discovered in Nanjiang County, is a Neolithic one.

1977

Yangbatai Site, discovered in Nanjiang County, is a Neolithic one.

1979

In March, Bazhong Memorial Hall of Sichuan-Shaanxi Revolutionary Base was renamed Sichuan-Shaanxi Revolutionary Base Museum.

1982

In December, Tongjiang County turned its Confucian Temple into the Military History Exhibition Hall of Sichuan-Shaanxi Revolutionary Base.

1984

Leiguzhai Site, discovered in Chunzai Township, Tongjiang County, is a Neolithic one.

1985

Wangping Tomb of Red Army Martyrs in Tongjiang was renamed Wangping Martyrs Cemetery.

1986

In July, Nuishui River Scenic Area in Tongjiang was officially opened to the public.

In October, Memorial Hall (stele) of Martyr Liu Bojian was completed.

1988

In January, the statue on the cliff in the south of Bazhong, the former site of the General Headquarters of the Fourth Front Red Army, the former site of the General Political Department of the Fourth Front Red Army, and the tomb of the Martyrs of the Fourth Front Red Army in Wangping were announced as "National Key Cultural Relics for Preservation".

1989

In August, Wangping Martyrs Cemetery was approved as a "National Key Memorial Building for Preservation" and "National Patriotism Education Demonstration Base".

1991

In January, Bazhou and Tongjiang were named "Famous Historical and Cultural Cities in Sichuan".

In July, Tongjiang County renamed Wangping Martyrs Cemetery the Fourth Front Red Army Wangping Martyrs Cemetery.

In September, the first Tongjiang Tremella Festival was held.

In the same year, Historical Relics Exhibition Hall of Dr. Yan Yangchu was built.

1992

In October, the Military History Exhibition Hall of Sichuan-Shaanxi Revolutionary Base was renamed Memorial Hall of the Former Site of General Headquarters of the Fourth Front Red Army.

Enyang Ancient Town was named "Famous Historical and Cultural Town in Sichuan".

1993

In July, the State Council approved of the establishment of

Bazhong Prefecture.

In September, Sichuan Provincial People's Government approved the establishment of Stele Forest for Soldiers and Officers with the Sichuan-Shaanxi Soviet Area in Bazhong South Niche Park.

In December, Mt. Guangwu Scenic Spot in Nanjiang County was approved as a provincial one.

1995

In April, Tongjiang County was named "China's Home to Tremella".

In May, Nuoshui River-Mt. Guangwu Scenic Spot was listed as one of Sichuan's top ten tourism projects to be developed and improved.

1998

In September, on his field trip to the Nuoshui River Scenic Area in Tongjiang County, Zhu Xuewen, geologist and chairman of the Cave Research Association of Chinese Geological Society called it home to karsts and caves in a true sense.

2000

In September, Sichuan-Shaanxi Revolutionary Base Museum was named "National Youth Education Base".

In December, Bazhong City was established in place of Bazhong Prefecture.

2001

In March, Bazhong's South Niche, North Niche, West Niche, and Cliff Statues in Shuining Temple were announced as "National Key Cultural Relics for Preservation".

In the same month, Wen Jiabao, member of the Standing Committee of the Political Bureau of the CPC Central Committee, Secretary of the Secretariat, and Vice Premier of the State Council, inspected Bazhong for research and guidance.

In June, Memorial Hall of the Former Site of General Headquarters of Fourth Front Red Army was named the "National Patriotiism Education Demonstration Base".

In December, Zhu Xuewen, Chairman of China Cave Association, visited Zhongfeng Cave on Nuoshui River, Tongjiang County, and called it "the World's Best Cave".

2002

In April, the first "2002 Sichuan·Bazhong Ba People's Culture and Art Festival" opened in Baiyuntai Community, Jiangbei Subdistrict.

In August, the Red Army Martyrs Cemetery was renamed Red Army Martyrs Cemetery of Sichuan-Shaanxi Revolutionary Base.

In October, Sichuan-Shaanxi Tourism Cooperation Meeting was held in Taoyuan Town, Nanjiang County.

In the same month, 2002 Mt. Guangwu Red Leaf Festival was held in Nanjiang.

In December, Mt. Micang Forest Park in Nanjiang was approved as a "National Forest Park".

2003

In October, the first China·Sichuan Mt. Guangwu Red Leaf Festival opened in Taoyuan, Nanjiang.

In December, Mt. Longshan in Pingchang Township was approved as a "National Forest Park".

In the same year, Bashan Guerrilla Memorial Hall got expanded.

2004

In January, Mt. Guangwu and Nuoshui River was approved as "National Key Scenic Area".

In September, Tremella Festival of Sichuan. Tongjiang, home to Karst Caves, opened in Tongjiang.

In December, Mt. Tianma in Bazhou District, Bazhong and Mt. Kongshan, Tongjiang were approved as "National Forest Parks".

In the same year, Bazhong was put on the list of "Red Tourism Area of Sichuan, Shaanxi and Chongqing" among the "National Key Red Tourism Areas", 30 national "Key Red Tourism Routes", and 100 national "Classic Red Tourism Scenic Spots".

2005

In April, Wen Jiabao, member of the Standing Committee of the Political Bureau of the CPC Central Committee and Premier of the State Council, inspected Bazhong.

In July, Memorial Hall of the Stele Forest for Soldiers and Officers with the Sichuan-Shaanxi Soviet Area was completed.

In October, the first Bazhong Tourism Development Meeting was held in Guangwushan Town, Nanjiang.

In the same month, Bazhong's Enyang, Bazhou District, got the title of "National Advanced Village and Town".

In November, Memorial Hall of Stele Forest for Soldiers and Officers with Sichuan-Shaanxi Soviet Area was named "National Patriotism Education Demonstration Base".

In the same month, Pingchang was rated as "National Culturally Advanced County".

2006

In June, Thousand-Buddha Crag Grottoes and Red Army Stone Slogan Group in Tongjiang were announced as "National Key Cultural Relics for Preservation".

In the same month, Bashan Porters' Song was included in the national intangible cultural heritage list.

In October, the first China·Sichuan Nanjiang Gazelle Festival opened in Nanjiang.

2007

In August, Nanjiang was rated as "China's Major Eco-Tourism County".

In September, Nanjiang was named "Home to Red Leaves in China".

In the same year, Bashan Guerrilla Memorial Hall was named "Sichuan Patriotism Education Base".

2008

In January, Li Keqiang, member of the Standing Committee of the Political Bureau of the CPC Central Committee and Vice Premier of the State Council, inspected Bazhong for research and guidance.

In April, Bazhong City was put on the list of the red-tourism theme of Sichuan-Shaanxi Soviet Area, one of the major three for tourism development by the province, and Sichuan-Shaanxi Revolutionary Base, one of the major six, and Sichuan-Shaanxi Soviet Area Tourist Route, one of the eight routes for red tourism.

In June, Bazhong traditional dancing of Fanshanjiaozi was included in the national intangible cultural heritage list.

In September, Pingchang's Jiangkou was approved as a "National Water Conservancy Scenic Area".

In October, Nanjiang was named "Home to Selenium-Enriched Tea in China".

In December, Bazhong's Enyang Town, Bazhou District, was named "Famous Town of Chinese History and Culture".

In the same year, Bazhong's Zengkou Town, Bazhong Disorict, was named "Home to Chinese Folk Culture and Art".

In the same year, Guangwushan Town, Nanjiang, was named "National Advanced Village and Town".

2009

In April, Mt. Guangwu Red Leaf Festival was listed as a major national festival.

In the same month, Bazhong was included in the Circle of "Key Routes for Three Kingdoms Cultural Tourism" in Sichuan, Shaanxi, Gansu and Chongqing at the launching ceremony.

2010

In February, Mt. Guangwu was approved as a national AAAA-level tourist attraction.

In the same month, Kongshan, Tongjiang, was rated as one of "Sichuan's Top 100 Eco-Tourism Townships".

2011

In July, Memorial Hall of the former site of General Headquarters of the Fourth Front Army was named "Sichuan's first clean government education bases".

In December, two villages including Yujin, Bazhong, received the title of "National Advanced Village and Town".

2012

In February, Nuojiang, Tongjiang, Sima, Pingchang, and Changchi, Nanjiang were rated as Provincial Ecological Townships.

In March, Bashan Guerrilla Memorial Hall opened.

In the same month, a 13-day "Micang Ancient Road" archaeological exploration and investigation was conducted by Sichuan Provincial Institute of Cultural Relics and Archaeology, together with other 15 units, National Museum included.

In May, the former site group of the Fourth Front Army General Hospital of the Chinese Workers' and Peasants' Red Army was named "Patriotism Education Base for National Health System".

In December, Micang Ancient Road entered *China's World Cultural Heritage Candidate List.*

2013

In January, Pingchang was named "National Leisure Agriculture and Rural Tourism Demonstration County" and "Sichuan Rural Tourism Demonstration County".

In February, both Wangping and Mt. Micang in Tongjiang and Nanjiang were approved as national AAAA-level tourist scenic areas.

In March, the first Sichuan's Bazhong-Pingchang Rural Tourism Culture Festival opened in Pingchang County.

From April to May, Nanjiang was named "China's Best Health-Leisure Tourism County" and "China's Blessed Land for Leisure, Vacation, Healthcare, and Elderly Care".

June witnessed the official opening of Bacheng Wangwangshan Sports Park, the first urban ecological sports theme park in Bazhong that integrates ecological protection, leisure and entertainment, sports and fitness, and sightseeing.

2014

In February, Baiyi Town, Pingchang, was named "Famous Town of Chinese History and Culture".

In April, the 5th Sichuan Rural Culture Tourism Festival was held in Pingchang.

In May, Nuoshui River and Mt. Fotou Scenic Spots were approved as national AAAA-level ones.

In June, Bazhong was named "Sichuan's Garden City".

In the same month, Enyang, Guangwushan, Shahe, Baiyi and Nuoshuihe Town, Bazhong, were named "National Ecological Towns".

In July, Bazhong was named a "Provincial Tourism Standardization Demonstration City", and Pingchang and Tongjiang were named "Provincial Tourism Standardization Demonstration Counties".

In September, Wangping Village, Shaxi Town, Tongjiang County, was named "National Ecological Cultural Village".

In December, Pingchang County was named "Home to Chinese Folk Culture and Art".

In the same month, Mt. Guangwu Scenic Area was approved as a "Provincial Tourist Resort".

2015

In January, Bazhong's Huahu Lake Water Conservancy Scenic Area was approved as a national one.

In February, Balingtai, Pingchang, was approved as a national AAAA-level tourist scenic area.

In the same month, two villages including Jinzi, Qingjiang Bazhong, were named "National Advanced Villages and Towns".

In April, the first "Bazhong Yunding" Tea Culture Tourism Festival was held on the Yunding Plaza, Yuandingzi Village, Nanjiang County.

In June, Bazhong was named "Home to Chinese Stone Carving Art".

In July, Bazhong's Mt. Micang, Mt. Kongshan, Mt. Zhenlong and Mt. Tianma National Forest Parks were rated as Sichuan's top 10 "Forest Healthcare Destinations".

In August, the first Pingchang Tea Culture Tourism Festival was held in Shilong Village, Luming Town.

In December, Nanjiang's Yubai, Hongguang Town, was named "National Ecological Cultural Village".

In the same month, Nanjiang's Zuimei Jade Lake and Colorful Long Beach and Pingchang's Sima Waterscape were approved as national AAAA-level tourist scenic areas.

2016

In February, Pingchang entered "Sichuan's First Major Rural Tourism Counties".

In July Bazhou District, Bazhong, was named "Home to Chinese Ballad Singers".

In October, Bazhong's Mt. South Niche and Shanshuihua Lake, Bazhong's Enyang Ancient Town, Bazhou District, Natural Bonsai in Tongjiang's Mt. Kongshan, and Nanjiang's Yunding Tea Farm were approved as national AAAA-level tourism scenic spots.

In November, Bazhong was named a "National Ecologically-Advanced City", and its Mt. Guangwu a national ecologically-advanced scenic spot.

In the same month, Bazhong's 10 villages, including Baiheshan, were on the list of traditional Chinese villages.

In the same year, Pingchang was rated as "National Top Ten Livable Counties".

2017

In January, 4 national forest parks including Mt. Micang were named "Sichuan's First National National Oxygen Bars".

In March, two forest Healthcare bases including Tongjiang's Changge Stone Forest were raised to the provincial level.

In May, a development promotion meeting for Sichuan's forest Healthcare industry was held in Nanjiang.

In July, Bazhong was named "National Sanitary City".

In August, Nanjiang's Jade Lake was approved as "National Water Conservancy Scenic Area".

In September, Nanjiang's Mt. Micang National Forest Park and Tongjiang's Stone Forest Scenic Spot in Changge Town were selected as "National Forest Health Base Pilot Units".

In October, Bazhong was named "National Forest City".

In November, Mt. Micang Forest Healthcare Base entered Sichuan's first "Forest Healthcare International Cooperation Demonstration Bases".

In the same month, Tongjiang's four villages including Zhongba, were named "National Advanced Villages and Towns".

In December, *Bazhong 's Regulations on the Protection of Red Army Cultural Relics* was approved for implementation by the Standing Committee of Sichuan Provincial People's Congress.

In the same month, the Fifth Plenary Session of the 4th Bazhong Municipal Party Committee proposed to vigorously develop eco-tourism and forest healthcare, speed up the establishment of a nationally renowned tourist destination and forest healthcare destination, and build a strong tourism economy.

Also in that month, five forest Healthcare bases including Bazhong's Mt. Zhanghuai in Enyang, were raised to the provincial level.

In the same year, Pingchang's Longwei, Yuntai Town, was named "China's Beautiful Leisure Village".

2018

In March, Pingchang's Baiyi Ancient Town and Mt. Huangjia Scenic Spots were approved as national AAAA-level tourist scenic areas.

In April, Nanjiang's Mt. Guangwu and Tongjiang's Mt. Kongshan were named "China's Most Beautiful Forest Towns".

In the same month, Mt. Guangwu-Nuoshui River Geopark was approved by UNESCO as a global one.

In October, Tongjiang's 8 forest healthcare bases including Bishan were raised to the provincial level.

In the same month, Pingchang's Shilong, Luming Town, was named "China's Beautiful Leisure Village".

In November, Bazhong was titled "2018 China National Tourism's Best Integrated Tourism Destination".

In December, *Grotto Protection Regulations in Bazhong* was approved by the Standing Committee of Sichuan People's Congress, the first ever local regulation regarding grotto relics for preservation in the province.

In the same month, Bazhong's 14 villages including Yuhuang, Xinglong Town, Enyang District, were put on the list of traditional Chinese villages.

In the same month, Bazhong's Enyang District was named a national practice and innovation base of "Clean Waters and Green Mountains as Invaluable Assets".

In the same month, Nanjiang was named "National Demonstration County for Ecological Development".

In the same month, Bazhong's Liujin Lake Water Conservancy Scenic Area was approved as a national one.

In the same month, Tongjiang's Maoyu was named "Famous Town of Chinese History and Culture".

In the same year, Bazhong's Colorful Niches Scenic Spot and Wanshou Healthcare Valley Scenic Spots respectively in Bazhou and Enyang Districts, were approved as national AAAA-level tourist scenic areas.

2019

In February, Bazhong's Mt. Tianma National Forest Park in Bazhou District, was named "China's Forest Healthcare Base".

In the same month, Pingchang's Longgang Town and Nanjiang's Yangba Town were named "Home to Chinese Folk Culture and Art".

In June, Bazhong's 5 red tourist routes became the recommended ones in Sichuan.

In August, Bazhong's theme route of Sichuan-Shaanxi Soviet Area was on the list of Sichuan's second ones.

In the same month, *Dreamland of Light and Mist*, China's first walk-immersed landscape night tour drama officially met its tourists.

In October, Tongjiang's 4 villages including Liyuanba, Nixi Town, were rated as "Sichuan's most beautiful ancient villages".

In the same month, the Grottoes in Shimen Temple were announced as "National Key Cultural Relics for Preservation".

In November, Tongjiang's Changge Stone Forest Scenic Spot was approved as a national AAAA-level tourist attraction.

2020

In May, Mt. Guangwu-Nuoshui River Global and Dagu Bingshan National Geoparks became "sister parks".

In June, Nanjiang's Mt. Micang Forest Healthcare Base was raised to the national level.

In June, Bazhong's four villages including Wanshou, Enyang District, were named "Sichuan's First Key Rural Tourism Villages"

In July, Sichuan's 11th (Summer) Rural Culture and Tourism Festival opened in Mt. Guangwu's Tieluba Square, Nanjiang.

In September, Nanjiang was named "Sichuan's Famous Tourism County".

In the same month, the ceremony of presenting flower baskets to the people's heroes in Sichuan was held at the Red Army Martyrs Cemetery in Sichuan-Shaanxi Revolutionary Base.

In the same month, Nanjiang's Xixiang, Chixi Town, was named "China's Beautiful Leisure Village".

In October, Pingchang was named and awarded as a national practice and innovation base for "Clean Waters and Green Mountains as Invaluable Assets".

In the same month, Bazhong was named "China's Capital of Climate and Healthcare".

In November, Nanjiang's 3 forest healthcare bases including Guangwuhegu were put on the list of "Pilot Construction Units for National Forest Healthcare Base".

In the same month, Enyang Ancient Town was selected as a "New Landmark of Bashu Cultural Tourism Corridor".

In the same month, Tongjiang's 5 villages including Wangping, Shaxi Town, were named "National Advanced Villages and Towns".

In December, Bazhong was identified as a "National Tourism Standardization Demonstration Unit".

In the same month, Bazhong's Mt. Guangwu Scenic Area was approved as a national AAAAA-level tourist attraction.

In the same month, Pingchang's Sima River Wetland Park was approved as a national one.

2021

In January, Mt. Jiuzhai in Bazhong Economic Development Zone and Pingchang's Dashi Fairy Tale Scenic Spots were approved as national AAAA-level tourist scenic areas.

In April, the large-scale situational night tour drama *The Legend of Enyang* was staged.

In June, 6 red scenic spots including Memorial Hall of former headquarters of the Fourth Front Red Army were included in the major route of "Surprise Soldiers into Sichuan · Heroes in War-Torn Years" with "100 Red Tourism Routes of the CPC's 100th Anniversary".

In July, 3 airlines, including Bazhong's Enyang and Beijing's

Daxing Airports, were selected as the first major national red tourism routes.

In the same month, the Red Army Martyrs Cemetery for Sichuan-Shaanxi Revolutionary Base was named "National Women's Patriotism Education Base".

In September, Bazhong released its city image logo, city tree and city flower.

In the same month, Tongjiang's Wangping, Shaxi Town, was named "Sichuan's Tourism Village".

In October, Tongjiang was named "National Demonstration County for Ecological Development".

In November, Bazhong's Mt. Guangwu-Nuoshui River Culture-Tourism Integration Development Demonstration Zone was established in Guangwushan Town, Nanjiang.

In the same month, Bazhong's first development meeting on culture, tourism and healthcare was held in Nanjiang.

In the same month, Nanjiang was named "Sichuan's Integrated Tourism Demonstration Area".

In the same month, Bazhong's fifth Party congress proposed a breakthrough in the development of its top-priority industry of culture, tourism and healthcare by implementing the strategy of strengthening itself through culture and tourism.

In December, Bazhong was rated as "China's Most Beautiful Ecological and Livable City".

In the same month, the promotional film "Poetic Landscape · Heroic Bazhong" officially appeared on the CCTV news channel, opening a new pattern for the publicity of its tourism.

In the same month, the 7th Mt. Guangwu Ice and Snow Festival opened.

2022

In January, China's first red-themed Zhenba-Guang'an Expressway (Wangping- Tongjiang Section) was officially opened to traffic.

In March, the first rapeseed flower festival called "Pastoral Enyang·Haishan Garden" opened in Liulin Modern Agricultural Park.

In June, the first Sichuan Nuoshui River International Karst Cave Festival opened at Tongjiang's Nuoshui Cave Scenic Spot.

In July, Bazhong's 10th Ba People's Culture and Art Festival opened in the City Gymnasium.

In the same month, the 7th "Bazhong Yunding" Tea Culture Tourism Festival opened in Nanjiang.

In the same month, Nanjiang's Guangwushan was named "Sichuan Famous Tourism Town", and its Xixiang was named "Sichuan Famous Tourism Village".

In August, the 2022 Open Tournament of Enyang Dragon Boat called "Row Across Sichuan" started in Enyang Dragon Boat Park.

In November, Tongjiang was named "Sichuan's Tourism County".

In the same month, the 20th Sichuan Mt. Guangwu International Red Leaf Festival opened in Nanjiang's Tieluba Square, Guangwushan Town.

In the same month, Bazhong's Wanshou, Xiabamiao Town, Enyang District, was named "China's Beautiful Leisure Village".

In the same month, Bazhong was named "National Ecologically-Advanced Demonstration Zone".

In December, Bazhou and Enyang Districts, together with Pingchang County, Bazhong, were named "Sichuan's Integrated Tourism Demonstration Zones".

巴中市文旅集团供图

米仓山旅游景区

Photo / Courtesy of Bazhong Cultural Tourism Group

Mt. Micang Tourist Scenic Area

第一篇

文化

Part 1

Culture

巴中市花 / 兰花（巴山春剑）
Bazhong's City Flower Orchid

第一章

巴人文化

巴人文化神秘而古老，是巴蜀文化和中华民族文明发展史的重要组成部分，具有“忠勇信义”的区域性文化精神特质。巴中处于巴人文化核心区域，是远古中华文明的发祥地之一。巴人文化历史悠久，内涵丰富，意蕴深邃，资源禀赋特色鲜明，遗址遗迹众多，有沙泥坪、月亮岩、擂鼓寨、断渠和阳八台等新石器时代遗址，有古遗址 170 余处、古建筑 280 余处、石窟寺及石刻 340 余处。米仓古道贯穿全境，留存有截贤岭、韩溪河、牟阳故城、巴峪关、得汉城、栾巴寺、黄柏林、长安古道等古道遗址和文化。有李白、杜甫、李商隐等诗人游历赋诗，有“巴山夜雨涨秋池”等千古佳句。有巴人脸谱、巴渝舞、巴山背二歌、翻山铰子、巴中皮影、茅山歌等活态形式的巴人文化名片。巴风、巴俗、巴语丰富多彩、鲜活生动。《巴文化普及读本》《巴中与巴文化》等巴人文化研究成果丰硕，先后举办的十届巴人文化艺术节享誉盛名。

张学金 / 摄　　Photo / Zhang Xuejin
巴渝舞　　**Bayu Dance**

Chapter 1

Ba People's Culture

Ba people's culture, ancient and mysterious, is an important part in the history of Bashu culture and Chinese civilization. Bazhong, located in the core area of this cultural atmosphere, is one of the birthplaces of ancient Chinese civilization. With long history, rich connotations, profound implications, distinctive resource endowments and numerous relics, there exist late Neolithic sites such as Moon Rock, Leigu Village, Broken Canal and Yangbatai, in addition to 170-plus ancient sites and ruins, over 280 ancient buildings, more than 340 cave temples and stone carvings. Where the Micang Ancient Road runs through, there are ancient road sites and cultures such as Sage-Buttonholing Ridge, Hanxi River, Mouyang Ancient City, Bayu Pass, Dehancheng Village, Luanba Temple, Golden Cypress Forest, and Chang'an Ancient Road. Poets such as Li Bai, Du Fu, and Li Shangyin visited here and left age-old beautiful lines ("You ask when I'll be home, but I don't know. All Bashan pools with autumn rain o'erflow", for instance). There are living cultural cards such as Ba people's facial makeup, Bayu dance, Bashan porters' song, traditional dancing of Fanshanjiaozi, Bazhong shadow play, and Maoshan song. And their customs, and dialect are also colorful and lively. The research on *Ba culture of Basic Culture Popularization Reader* and *Bazhong and Ba Culture* has borne fruit. Well-known are the ten Ba People's Culture and Art Festivals held successively, and the Center for Ba Culture.

巴人文化艺术节

巴人文化艺术节是巴中市的文化节日，是泛巴区域文化交流、经济合作、文旅融合的艺术节活动。活动旨在担当文化传承使命、搭建交流互鉴平台，共同促进巴文化繁荣发展。自 2002 年巴中市委、市人民政府开始举办巴人文化艺术节以来，接续举办了十届。

夏雨 / 摄
第十届巴人文化艺术节开幕式

Photo / Xia Yu
Opening Ceremony of the 10th Ba People's Culture and Art Festival

Ba People's Culture and Art Festival

This festival, an artistic activity in the pan-Ba area of cultural exchange, economic cooperation and integration of culture and tourism, is meant for the mission of cultural inheritance, a platform for the exchange and mutual learning, co-promotion of the prosperity and development of Ba culture. Since 2002, Ba People's Cultural and Art Festival has been held for 10 times running under the Bazhong Municipal Party Committee and People's Government.

沙泥坪遗址

沙泥坪遗址位于巴中市巴州区大和乡界牌村和通江县杨柏镇沙泥坪村交界处的缓坡地上，为新石器时代遗址。遗址出土有夹砂褐陶、灰陶、黑陶片和石器残片等。石器以砾石器为主，器形有石锛、石斧、刮削器等。陶器以夹砂陶为主，纹饰有斜方格纹等，器形以罐形较多。该遗址为研究大巴山古人类活动提供了珍贵的实物资料。

Shaniping Site

This site, located on a gentle slope at the junction of Jiepai and Shaniping Villages, Dahe, Bazhou District and Yangbai Town, respectively in Bazhong and Tongjiang Counties, is a Neolithic one, where some fragments of sandy brown, gray, black pottery and stoneware were unearthed. The latter was mainly of gravel shaped like adze, axe, scraper and the like. The pottery was mainly that of sand, decorated with oblique grid patterns, and mostly shaped like pots. This site provides extremely precious physical data for the study of ancient human activities in the Daba Mountains.

上图　巴中市史志馆供图
沙泥坪遗址出土石器
下图　巴中市史志馆供图
沙泥坪遗址

Above Photo / Bazhong History Museum
Stoneware Unearthed from Shaniping Site
Below Photo / Bazhong History Museum
Shaniping Site

月亮岩遗址

月亮岩遗址位于巴中市恩阳区渔溪镇酒店社区，为新石器时代遗址。遗址共出土磨制石斧 10 件、砍砸石器 2 件，采集陶片 170 余件。陶片中有夹砂陶、泥质灰陶，以灰色居多，褐色次之，并有少量红陶。纹饰有波浪纹、绳纹，附加堆纹、戳纹、菱形纹、刻划纹及素面等。

Moon Rock Site

This site, located in the Jiudian Community of Yuxi Town, Enyang District, Bazhong City, is one of Neolithic stone tools, where 10 polished stone axes, 2 chopped and smashed stone tools, and more than 170 pottery pieces have been unearthed. These pieces include those of sand and grey mud, followed by brown, and red. Their patterns are of wave, rope, additional grain, stamping, rhomboid, scribing and plainness.

上图　张学金 / 摄
月亮岩遗址
下图　巴中市史志馆供图
月亮岩遗址出土陶片

Above Photo / Zhang Xuejin
Moon Rock Site
Below Photo / Courtesy of Bazhong History Museum
Pottery Shards Unearthed from Moon Rock Site

断渠遗址

断渠遗址位于南江县城郊，为新石器时代遗址，有洞穴及磨制、石制工具作坊遗址，出土石锄、石斧等新石器时代石器和陶片。遗址现辟为断渠公园，由山、水、林、石、渠、洞组成八大景观，60 余个景点。

Broken Canal Site

This site, also a Neolithic one, located on the outskirts of Nanjiang, includes caves and grinding and stone tool workshop sites, and Neolithic stone tools and pottery pieces such as stone hoes and stone axes have been unearthed. Now it is turned into a park, made up of eight landscapes, and 60-plus scenic spots, such as mountains, water, forests, rocks, canals and caves.

上图　张学金 / 摄
断渠遗址
下图　丁伟 / 摄
阳八台遗址

Above Photo / Zhang Xuejin
Broken Canal Site
Below Photo / Ding Wei
Yangbatai Site

擂鼓寨遗址

擂鼓寨遗址位于通江县春在镇擂鼓寨村，为新石器时代遗址。遗址共出土石器、陶器等 20685 件（片），其中石器及石器半成品 812 件，陶器 19873 件（片）。陶器主要有罐、尊形器、瓶、盆、钵、杯、碗、器盖等。石器以磨制为主，主要有斧、锛、凿、镞、矛、石球、盘状器等。器形主要有肩石锄、肩石斧、刮削器、砍砸器、尖状器。细石器（4 件）均为刮削器。

Leigu Village Site

This site,located in Leigu Village, Chunzai Town, Tongjiang County, is one of the Neolithic Site. a total of 20,685 items (pieces) of stone tools and pottery have been unearthed, including 812 items of (semi-)finished stone tools and 19,873 items (pieces) of pottery. Pottery contains jars, zun-shaped utensils, bottles, basins, bowls, cups, bowls, lids and so on. Stone tools are mainly ground ones, including axes, adzes, chisels, arrowheads, spears, stone balls, discs, etc. The main shapes of the tools are shoulder stone hoes, shoulder stone axes, scrapers, choppers, and pointed tools. The microliths (4 items) are all scrapers.

上图　巴中市史志馆供图
擂鼓寨遗址出土陶片
下图　何嗣猛 / 摄
擂鼓寨遗址

Above Photo / Courtesy of Bazhong History Museum
Pottery Sherds Unearthed from Leigu Village Site
Below Photo / He Simeng
Leigu Village Site

Micang Ancient Road

Micang Ancient Road, with over 240 kilometer's long, located along the Qinling Mountains, the China's South to North geographical dividing line. It starts from Shaanxi's Hanzhong in the north, down to Nanzheng, Sichuan's Nanjiang, mainly through Mt. Micang, and ends in Bazhong. As one of the three well-known ones, the other two being Jinniu and Litchi Roads in Sichuan, it is the key north-south link of civilizations in the Yellow and Yangtze River Basins, in terms of significant military channel and transportation route for food materials in Chinese history, hence the name of "living fossil in the history of transportation in China and even the world". In 2012, this road has entered *China's World Cultural Heritage Candidate List.*

米仓古道

米仓古道位于中国南北地理分界线的秦岭，北起陕西汉中，经陕西南郑入四川南江，主线越米仓山，南抵巴中，全长 240 多千米，是中国最早的国道，与金牛道、荔枝道并称三大古蜀道之一，是历史上极为重要的北连黄河流域文明、南连长江流域文明的军事通道和粮食物资运输要道，被誉为“中国乃至世界交通史上的活化石”。2012 年，米仓古道入选《中国世界文化遗产预备名单》。

上图　巴中市文旅集团供图
南江米仓古道碑沟口
下图　何嗣猛 / 摄
通江米仓古道上阎王碥栈道

Above Photo / Courtesy of Bazhong Cultural Tourism Group
Daobeikou of Micang Ancient Road, Nanjiang
Below Photo / He Simeng
Danger Spot Section of Micang Ancient Road, Tongjiang

巴灵台旅游景区

巴灵台旅游景区位于平昌县灵山镇，是国家 AAAA 级旅游景区。景区奇峰独绝，秀美险峻，建筑依山而建，古朴典雅，集儒教、道教、佛教于一山，有观音庙、牛王庙、大佛殿、灵宫殿等 9 座庙宇及 1 座斋堂。景区北门前有清乾隆房山知县吴道凝（平昌籍）题写“巴灵台”三字。景区所在的灵山镇巴灵台社区为中国传统村落。

Balingtai Tourist Scenic Area

Balingtai, a national AAAA-level tourist area, is located in Lingshan Town, Pingchang County, where the peaks are unique, beautiful and precipitous, and the simple and elegant buildings constructed along the mountain. As a gathering of Confucianism, Taoism and Buddhism in one place, it owns 9 temples such as Guanyin, Niuwang, Big Buddha, and Linggong, in addition to one vegetarian hall. On the front of its north gate are the three Chinese characters of Ba Ling Tai by Wu Daoning (a native of Pingchang), magistrate of Fangshan County, during the reign of Qianlong Emperor of the Qing Dynasty. Balingtai Community, Lingshan Town, where this area is located, is a traditional Chinese village.

上图　平昌县文广旅局供图
平昌巴灵台旅游景区
下图　平昌县灵山镇供图
吴道凝题写的“巴灵台”

Above Photo / Pingchang of Bureau of Culture, Radio and Tourism
Balingtai Tourist Scenic Spot
Below Photo / Courtesy of Lingshan Town, Pingchang
Ba Ling Tai Inscribed by Wu Daoning

平梁城遗址

平梁城遗址位于巴中市巴州区平梁镇平梁山顶，地形险峻，四面绝壁，上有良田清泉。汉将军严颜定汉昌曾在此储粮屯兵。南宋淳祐十一年（1251），都统张实砌石壁为城抗击蒙军，抚平梁州。现存有城墙、寨门及严公台、张必禄墓、真武宫庙、结喜寺庙等遗址。

上图　张学金 / 摄
平梁城遗址
下图　谭守学 / 摄
平梁古城石碑

Above Photo / Zhang Xuejin
Pingliang City Site
Below Photo / Tan Shouxue
Stele at Pingliang Ancient City

Pingliang City Site

At this site, located atop Mt. Pingliang, Bazhong's Pingliang Town, Bazhou District, is steep in terrain and surrounded by cliffs but with fertile fields and clear springs, where General Yan Yan had once stored grain and stationed troops; and in the eleventh year of Chunyou in the Southern Song Dynasty (1251), General Commander Zhang Shi had a stone wall built against the Mongolian army in defense of Liangzhou Prefecture. There exist now ruins such as city wall, walled gate, Terrace of General Yan Yan, Zhang Bilu's Tomb, Zhenwu Palace and Jiexi Temple.

牟阳故城遗址

牟阳故城遗址位于巴中市文旅新区米仓山大坝牟家山之南。始建于商周，毁于民国。牟阳故城自古便为商旅云集和兵家必争之地，鼎盛时期居烟户，兴私塾、屠场、酿酒作坊、客栈，关帝庙殿宇恢宏，香火兴盛。

Mouyang Ancient City Site

This ancient city, situated south of Moujiashan, in Mt. Micang's Dam, Bazhong's Cultural Tourism New Area, established in the Shang and Zhou period and got ruined in the Republic of China. It had ever since been vied for by all military strategists. During its heyday, Mouyang had been settled, with a private school, slaughter house, brewery, and tavern, in addition to a magnificent Guanyu Temple where incense so flourished.

张学金 / 摄
牟阳故城遗址

Photo / Zhang Xuejin
Mouyang Ancient City Site

小宁城遗址

小宁城遗址位于平昌县江口街道小宁寨，四面绝壁，三面环水，仅东门连通陆路。南宋淳祐五年（1245），都统张实于此筑城，于淳祐九年（1249）竣工。外筑午城，内筑子城，东南西北四门城楼高悬。现东门（朝阳门）、西门、北门、重禧门及城墙保存较为完好。

Xiaoning City Site

Located in Pingchang's Xiaoning Village, Jiangkou Street, it is surrounded by cliffs on all sides and water on three, and only the east gate is connected to land. In the fifth year of Chunyou (1245) of the Southern Song Dynasty, General Commander Zhang Shi had the city built, and completed four years after.With Wucheng built outside, and sub-cities inside, all its four tower gates stood high in each direction, and even now the East Gate(Chaoyang Gate), West Gate, North Gate, Chongxi Gate and Walls are stay relatively well preserved.

王建华 / 摄
小宁城遗址

Photo / Wang Jianhua
Xiaoning City Site

Dehan City Site

Also known as Anji Village, it located in Tongjiang's Dehancheng Village, Yong'an Town, facing streams on three sides and steep on four sides. The terrain here as the throat of Qin and Shu (Shaanxi and Sichuan at present) has been the battleground for military strategists of all dynasties. In the early Han Dynasty, Xiao He used it as the road for transporting military food. At the end of the Southern Song Dynasty, Yu Jie had it built, as one of Sichuan's eight battlefield sites against the Yuan invaders. During the time of Sichuan-Shaanxi Soviet Area, it was the main logistics support base for the Fourth Front Red Army and Sichuan-Shaanxi Soviet Government in addition to Northwest Revolutionary Military Committee, Red Army Radio Station, Pengyang Military School (named after the then peasant movement leaders of Peng Pai and Yang Yin), Security Bureau and Mint established here.

得汉城遗址

得汉城又名安辑寨，位于通江县永安镇得汉城村，三面临涧，四面陡峭。地势险峻，扼秦蜀咽喉、据巴西要冲，为历代兵家必争之地。汉初，萧何据此以通饷道。南宋末，余玠创筑得汉城，为南宋四川抗元八柱之一。川陕苏区时期，为红四方面军和川陕省苏维埃政府主要后勤保障基地，曾在此设立西北革命军事委员会、红军电台、彭杨军事学校、保卫局、造币厂等机构。

上图　杨正保 / 摄 Above Photo / Yang Zhengbao
得汉城石刻 **Carvings on Dehan City**
下图　曾建飞 / 摄 Below Photo / Zeng Jianfei
得汉城遗址 **Dehan City Site**

第二章

石窟文化

巴中是中国石刻艺术之乡。巴中石窟历史悠久，始凿于隋代，盛凿于唐代，后经历代增凿形成。巴中石窟与两京、河西等北方石窟一脉相承，是吸收融合外来文化的典范，分布广泛，内容丰富，造型精美，既有佛家气象，又有自然之美。石窟由精湛的雕刻技艺在悬崖石壁上连片雕凿而成，装饰华丽，色彩变幻多样，是中国隋唐时期佛教石窟的重要代表作品，享有“盛唐彩雕全国第一”的美誉，是研究历史、文化、艺术、宗教的重要实物资料。巴中市现存石窟造像 223 处、800 余龛、15000 余尊。其中，全国重点文物保护单位 4 处 7 点（南龛石窟、北龛石窟、西龛石窟、水宁寺石窟、通江千佛岩石窟、白乳溪石窟、石门寺石窟）、省级文物保护单位 16 处，市县（区）级文物保护单位 28 处。颁布四川省第一部石窟文物保护领域的地方性法规《巴中市石窟保护条例》。

内图　张学金 / 摄
南龛摩崖造像群
外图　张学金 / 摄
南龛摩崖造像之西方净土（局部）

Inside Photo / Zhang Xuejin
South Niche Cliff Statue Group
Outside Photo / Zhang Xuejin
Western Pure Land of South Niche Cliff Statue Group (Partial)

Chapter 2

Grotto Culture

Bazhong is home to the Chinese stone carving art, where the history of grottoes can be traced back to far back as the Sui, prime-time Tang, and nonstop following dynasties. The grottoes here, of the same origin as those in Luoyang, Chang'an, and Hexi Corridor in North China, are a model for absorbing and integrating alien cultures. Widely distributed, rich in content and exquisite in shape, they are of both Buddhist air and natural beauty. With outstanding characteristics, exquisite skills, gorgeous decoration, and varied colors, Bazhong Grottoes are important representative works of Buddhism in China's Sui and Tang Dynasties, hence the name of "No.1 Color Sculpture of the Sui and Tang Dynasties in China" due to its important physical evidence for the study of Chinese history, culture and religion. There exist here 223 grotto statues, over 800 caves and 15,000 statues, respectively. Among them, there are 4 national key cultural relics for preservation with 7 points (grottoes in South Niche , North Niche, West Niche, Shuining Temple, Tongjiang's Thousand Buddhas, Bairu Stream and Shimen Temple), and provincial cultural relics for preservation. There are 16 and 28 cultural relics for preservation, respectively at the provincial, city- and county- (district-) levels. *Regulations on the Protection of Grottoes in Bazhong City*, the first local one in Sichuan, has been promulgated.

南龛石窟

南龛摩崖造像位于巴中市城南南龛山腰，为第三批全国重点文物保护单位。造像始凿于初唐，盛唐和中晚唐亦多有开凿，宋及民国有少量造像。造像内容丰富，造型精美，色彩鲜艳，保存完好，堪称“国之瑰宝”。现存造像 176 龛（其中瘗窟 24 龛）、造像 2700 余尊、题记 15 幅、碑碣 79 通。造像聚集了佛教各派的风格，主要内容有释迦牟尼佛、三世佛、弥勒佛、菩提瑞像、双头瑞像、地藏菩萨、观音菩萨、鬼子母以及经幢和瘗窟等。

1 张学金 / 摄
南龛摩崖造像之毗卢遮那佛
2 张学金 / 摄
南龛摩崖造像之西方净土变
3 张学金 / 摄
南龛摩崖造像之双头瑞像
4 张学金 / 摄
南龛摩崖造像之数珠手观音

1. Photo / Zhang Xuejin
Vairocana Buddha Statue on South Niche Cliff
2. Photo / Zhang Xuejin
Sukhavati Statue on South Niche Cliff
3. Photo / Zhang Xuejin
Double-Headed Buddha on South Niche Cliff
4. Photo / Zhang Xuejin
Rosary Guanyin on South Niche Cliff

1

2

3

4

South Niche Grottoes

Located on the mountainside of Mt. South Niche in the southern suburb of Bazhong, the cliff statues are among the third national key cultural relics for preservation. They began in the early Tang Dynasty, and many were cut at its prime, middle and late periods. A few of them were done in the Song Dynasty and the Republic of China. Rich in content, exquisite in shape, bright in color and well preserved, they are worthy "national treasures". There are 176 niches of statues (including 24 tomb grottoes), over 2,700 statues, 15 inscriptions, and 79 steles. The statues gather various styles of Buddhism, mainly Sakyamuni Buddha, Triratna, Maitreya Buddha, Putiri Statue, Double-Headed Buddha, Ksitigarbha Bodhisattva, Avalokitesvara Bodhisattva, Hariti, Dharani Pillars and Tomb Grottoes.

西龛石窟

西龛摩崖造像位于巴中市城西西龛山的佛爷湾、流杯池、龙日寺，为第五批全国重点文物保护单位。造像始凿于隋，唐代作品较多。造像技艺熟练，多彩多姿，装饰华丽。布局灵活多样，龛窟多为方形、拱形，龛柱、楣多刻缠枝纹、忍冬纹、狮等。现存造像 92 龛，主要内容有释迦牟尼佛、弥勒佛、阿弥陀佛、飞天、伎乐等。

West Niche Grottoes

The cliff statues here, located in Foyewan (also called West Niche Temple), Liubeichi and Longri Temple in West Niche, in the western suburb of Bazhong, are among the fifth national key cultural relics for preservation. These works, skilled, colorful and ornately decorated, started in the Sui Dynasty, but more of them were done in the Tang Dynasty. Their layout is flexible and diverse; most niches are square or arched, and the pillars and lintels are carved with tangled branches, honeysuckle patterns, and lions. There are 92 ones in existence, mainly including Sakyamuni Buddha, Maitreya Buddha, Amitabha Buddha, Flying Apsaras, and Musicians and Dancers.

上图　张敬伟 / 摄
西龛佛爷湾摩崖造像
下图　张学金 / 摄
西龛佛爷湾摩崖造像群（局部）

Above Photo / Zhang Jingwei
West Niche Cliff Statues at Foyewan
Below Photo / Zhang Xuejin
West Niche Cliff Statue Group (Partial) at Foyewan

张敬伟 / 摄　　Photo / Zhang Jingwei
北龛摩崖造像　　**North Niche Cliff Statues**

北龛石窟

北龛摩崖造像位于巴中市城北苏山坪，为第五批全国重点文物保护单位。造像始凿于初唐，现存造像34龛、348尊，主要内容有七佛、释迦牟尼佛、弥勒佛、菩提瑞像、二佛并坐、三世佛、释迦老君并坐、药师佛与观音、地藏菩萨、观音立像和清代碑刻等。其中，7号龛药师经变相最具特色，内容极为丰富。

North Niche Grottoes

The cliff statues here, located in Sushanping in the northern suburb of Bazhong City, are among the fifth national key cultural relics for preservation. They began in the early Tang Dynasty with 34 niches and 348 in existence, which mainly includes Seven Buddhas, Sakyamuni Buddha, Maitreya Buddha, Bodhirui Statue, Two Buddhas sitting abreast, Triratna, Sakyamuni sitting with Lord Lao Zi, Medicine Buddha and Avalokitesvara Bodhisattva, Ksitigarbha, statue of Avalokitesvara Bodhisattva and inscriptions of the Qing Dynasty. Among them, the statue of Medicine Buddha transformation in No. 7 Niche is the most distinctive and rich in content.

通江千佛岩石窟

通江千佛岩石窟位于通江县城西千佛岩，为第六批全国重点文物保护单位。为唐代造像，雕刻精细，造型丰满，线条流畅。龛窟形式有单层方形龛、双层方形龛、外方内圆龛、屋形龛。现存造像 54 龛、3000 余尊，浮雕石塔 1 座，造像题记 4 幅，重妆题记 2 幅，碑刻 2 通，以释迦牟尼、观世音、大势至为主像，以力士、供养人、乐伎为伴像。浅浮雕供养人在四川摩崖造像中极为少见，浮雕七级宝塔人字形斗拱和直斗重叠组合，除西安大雁塔门楣上的线刻图外，此处亦有。

何嗣猛 / 摄
通江千佛岩石窟之七级宝塔浮雕

Photo / He Simeng
Relief of Seven-Story Stupa in Tongjiang's Thousand-Buddha Crag

Thousand-Buddha Crag Grottoes in Tongjiang

These grottoes, located in the western suburb of Tongjiang County, are among the sixth national key cultural relics for preservation. They are statues of the Tang Dynasty, with fine carvings, plump shapes and smooth lines. The forms of niches are either single-layer square, double-layer square, outer-square inner-circular, or house-shaped. There are 54 niches with over 3,000 statues, one stone tower in relief, 4 statues with inscriptions, 2 inscriptions on recolour, and 2 steles with inscriptions. The main statues are Sakyamuni, Avalokitesvara, and Mahasthamaprapta accompanied by mallas, donors, and musicians and dancers. Among them, the bas-relief donors are extremely rare in Sichuan's cliff statues; as for the relief sculptures of the seven-story pagoda with herring bone-shaped bucket arches and straight buckets overlapped, this is the only one besides the line engraving on the lintel of the Big Wild Goose Pagoda in Xi'an.

水宁寺石窟

水宁寺摩崖造像位于巴中市巴州区水宁寺镇，为第五批全国重点文物保护单位。造像始凿于隋，盛于唐，多为唐代造像，造像保存极好，雕刻精美，内容丰富。现存造像 38 龛、316 尊，主要内容有药师三尊、释迦说法、释迦弥勒并坐、观音善财龙女、天龙八部等。石窟所在地七彩佛龛景区为国家 AAAA 级旅游景区，水宁寺镇新庙村为全国文明村镇。

左图　张学金 / 摄
水宁寺摩崖造像群（局部）
右图　张学金 / 摄
水宁寺摩崖造像之药师三尊

Grottoes in Shuining Temple

The cliff statues here, located in Shuiningsi Town, Bazhou District, Bazhong, are among the fifth national key cultural relics for preservation. They began in the Sui and flourished in the Tang Dynasties, when most of them were made, and now stay well preserved, beautifully carved and rich in content. Of the 38 niches and 316 statues in existence, there are three Medicine Buddhas, Preaching Sakyamuni Buddha, Sakyamuni sitting with Avalokitesvara, Sudhana, and Demi-Gods and Semi-Devils. Colorful Focan, where the grottoes are located, is a national AAAA-level tourist scenic area, and Xinmiao, Shuiningsi Town, is one of the national advanced villages and towns.

Left Photo / Zhang Xuejin
Cliff Statue Group in Shuining Temple (Partial)
Right Photo / Zhang Xuejin
Three Medicine Buddhas on Shuining Temple Cliff

第三章

红色文化

巴中是革命老区，红色文化璀璨。巴中是川陕革命根据地的中心和首府、四川和川陕革命老区唯一的全国革命老区重点城市，川陕苏区是中华苏维埃共和国的第二个大区域，红色文化资源丰富。有全国最大红军烈士陵园、最大红军石刻标语群、最大红军将帅碑林。有不可移动革命文物 397 处 511 点，其中全国重点文物保护单位 3 处 81 点，省级文物保护单位 34 处 70 点，市级文物保护单位 17 处，县级文物保护单位 137 处，一般文物 206 处。有可移动革命文物 3 万余件（套）。巴中红色遗址遗迹和纪念场馆丰富多样，有革命类博物馆、纪念馆 9 个，革命文物资源较集中的革命旧址群 7 个。红色文化资源涵盖川陕苏区党政军群机关旧址、战役战斗遗址、红军石刻标语、红军烈士陵园、纪念场馆等，以保存较好的遗址、原物居多，更有红四方面军“十六字”训词等精神类红色资源。先后创作开发有戏剧《望红台》《小军号》《周永开》，图书《刘伯坚》《红色故事连环画》，体验课程“为烈士墓碑五星描红”和微党课《巴山女红军》等红色文艺作品。颁布地方性法规《巴中市红军文物保护条例》。

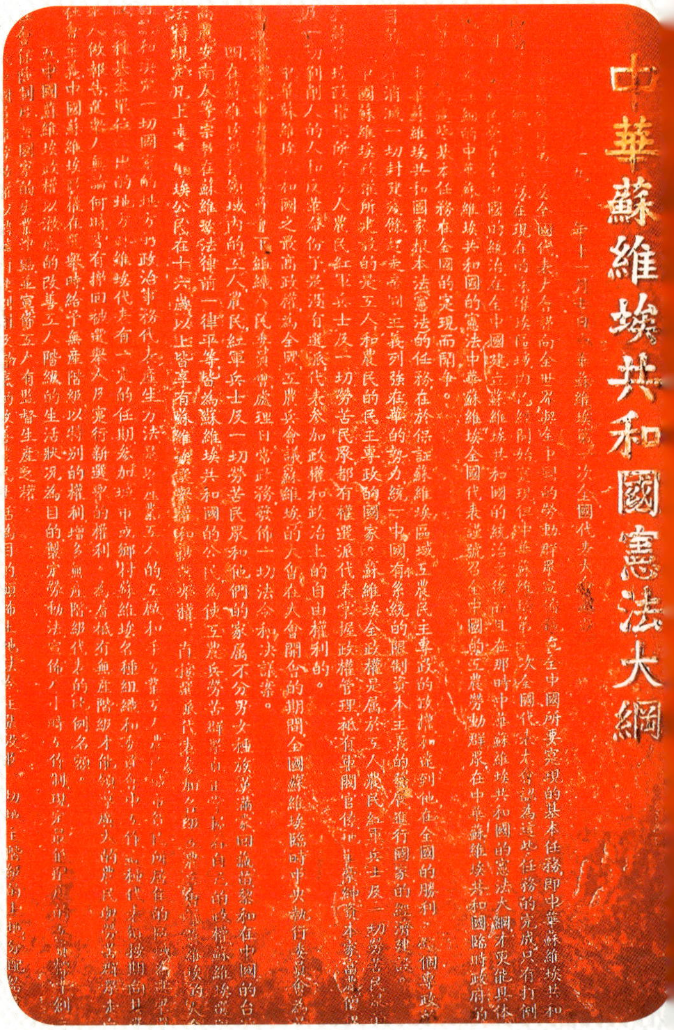

程林斌供图
《中华苏维埃共和国宪法大纲》石刻文献（局部）
Photo / Cheng Linbin
Stone-Carved *Constitution Outline of Chinese Soviet Republic* (Partial)

Chapter 3

Revolutionary Culture

程林斌供图
《川陕省苏维埃政府布告》石刻文献（局部）
Photo / Cheng Linbin
Stone-Carved Document of Proclamation of Sichuan-Shaanxi Soviet Government (Partial)

Bazhong is an old revolutionary base, shining pearl of revolutionary culture, center and Capital of Sichuan-Shaanxi Revolutionary Base, China's only Key City in Sichuan's and Sichuan-Shaanxi's Old Revolutionary Bases and second largest area of the Chinese Soviet Republic as well. It boasts the largest Red Army Martyrs Cemetery, Stone Slogan Group, and Stele Forest for Red Army Soldiers and Officers; 511 immovable revolutionary cultural relics in 397 places, of which 3 national key cultural relics for preservation with 81 points, 34 provincial cultural relics for preservation with 70 points, 17 municipal-level cultural relics for preservation, and 137 county-level cultural relics for preservation, in addition to 206 ordinary ones. It has over 30,000 (set) movable cultural relics, 9 revolutionary museums and memorial halls, and 7 revolutionary sites with their relatively concentrated cultural relics resources. Its red cultural relics resources include such sites as those of the Party, government and army in the Sichuan-Shaanxi Soviet Area, battle sites, Red Army's slogans, Red Army Martyrs Cemetery, and various memorial venues, most of them and original objects of which stay intact, in addition to spiritual resources such as "16-Character Precept" by the Fourth Front Red Army, Bazhong has successively created and developed such dramas as *Waiting Terrace for Red Army*, *Small Bugle*, and *Zhou Yongkai*, books as *Liu Bojian* and *Illustrated Revolutionary Stories*, experience courses like Reddening the Five Stars on Revolutionary Martyrs' Tombstones and micro-Party classes like *Bashan Red Army Women*, and promulgated its *Regulations on Red Army Cultural Relics Protection in Bazhong City*.

程聪 / 摄
“赤化全川” 红军石刻标语

Photo / Cheng Cong
Red Army's Stone Carved Slogan of "A Revolutionary Sichuan"

化
赤

上左图　肖裕孟 / 摄
巴中市文旅新区两河口镇八一希望学校
上右图　肖裕孟供图
红军入川第一镇石碑
下图　杨卫民 / 摄
红军入川第一镇——巴中市文旅新区两河口镇

Top Left Photo / Xiao Yumeng
Bayi Hope School, Lianghekou Town
Top Right Photo / Xiao Yumeng
Stone Tablet at Sichuan's First Town Red Army Entered
Below Photo / Yang Weimin
Lianghekou, Sichuan's First Town Red Army Entered

红军入川第一镇——两河口镇

1932 年 12 月 17 日，红四方面军以红七十三师二一七团为先遣队，翻越巴山，向川北挺进，于 18 日占领川陕边境交界重镇——通江县两河口。21 日，红四方面军全部进抵通江县境，建立了红军入川后的第一个工农革命政权——两河口乡苏维埃政府。之后以通江为中心，在两年半的时间里，创建了川陕革命根据地，成为全国第二大苏区。两河口镇以“红军入川第一镇”被载入史册。

Lianghekou, the First Town in Sichuan Where the Red Army Entered

On December 17, 1932, the Fourth Front Red Army, with its 217th Regiment of 73rd Division as the advance team, crossed Mt. Bashan and entered the north of Sichuan. On the 18th, it conquered Lianghekou of Tongjiang County, a key place at the junction of Sichuan and Shaanxi. On the 21st, all the Fourth Front Red Army arrived, and established Lianghekou Town Soviet Government, the first revolutionary regime of workers and peasants in Sichuan. With Tongjiang as the center, in two and a half years, the Sichuan-Shaanxi Revolutionary Base was founded, and became the second largest Soviet area across China. Lianghekou Town has ever since been recorded in history as "the first town in Sichuan where the Red Army entered".

张学金 / 摄
川陕革命根据地红军烈士陵园

Photo / Zhang Xuejin
Red Army Martyrs Cemetery of Sichuan-Shaanxi Revolutionary Base

左图　川陕革命根据地红军烈士陵园管理局供图
英烈纪念墙
右上图　张学金 / 摄
铁血丹心主题雕塑
右下图　通江县地方志办公室供图
张琴秋设计并题字碑名的烈士墓碑

Left Photo / Courtesy of Red Army Martyrs Cemetery Administration for Sichuan-Shaanxi Revolutionary Base Area
Martyrs' Memorial Wall
Top Right Photo / Zhang Xuejin
Sculpture for War Heroes
Bottom Right Photo / Courtesy of Tongjiang Local Record Office
Martyrs' Tombstone Designed and Inscribed by Zhang Qinqiu

川陕革命根据地红军烈士陵园

川陕革命根据地红军烈士陵园位于通江县沙溪镇王坪村，是全国重点文物保护单位、全国重点烈士纪念建筑物保护单位、全国爱国主义教育示范基地、全国妇女爱国主义教育基地、四川省青少年社会实践教育基地、全国 100 个红色旅游经典景区和 30 条红色精品旅游线路之一，也是国家 AAAA 级旅游景区。陵园由铁血丹心广场、千秋大道、陵园核心区、散葬墓区、纪念馆等部分组成，分布有铁血丹心主题雕塑、英勇烈士纪念碑、红军烈士集墓区、无名烈士纪念园、英烈纪念墙、红四方面军总医院旧址群、“赤化全川”石刻标语等景点。陵园安葬英烈 25048 名，是全国安葬红军烈士最多、规模最大的红军烈士陵园。其中，红军烈士集墓区集中安葬红军烈士 7823 名，是中国唯一一处红军为战友修建的陵园，也是全国最大的红军烈士集墓。陵园所在地王坪村为全国生态文化村、全国文明村镇、国家森林乡村、天府旅游名村、四川省首批乡村旅游重点村。

Red Army Martyrs' Cemetery of Sichuan-Shaanxi Revolutionary Base

This base, located in Tongjiang's Wangping Village, Shaxi Town, is a national key cultural relics and martyr memorial building for preservation, a national base for patriotism education demonstration and women's patriotism education, one for Sichuan Youth Social Practice Education, one of China's 100 classic red tourism scenic spots, 30 red tourist routes, and a national AAAA-level tourist scenic area as well. The cemetery consists of War Heroes Square, Qianqiu Avenue, Core Area, Separate Burial Area, and Memorial Hall, which covers spots such as War Heroes' Statue, Monument to Red Army Martyrs, Group Burial Area for Red Army Martyrs, Memorial Garden of Unknown Martyrs, Memorial Wall for Heroic Martyrs, Former Site Group of Fourth Front Army's General Hospital and Stone-Carved Slogan of "A Revolutionary Sichuan". With 25,048 buried here, it makes China's largest cemetery for the Red Army martyrs. Among them, 7,823 have received a centralized burial, the only and largest one built by the Red Army personnel for their comrades-in-arms in China. Wangping, where the cemetery is located, is a national ecological, cultural, advanced, and forest village, and a famous Sichuan tourism village among the first key ones for rural tourism.

1　张学金 / 摄

“争取苏维埃中国”红军石刻标语

2　席凯供图

川陕苏区钱币

3　李杰供图

恩阳古镇红军石刻标语

4　红四方面军总指挥部旧址纪念馆供图

通江县杨柏镇太平社区红军墨书文献

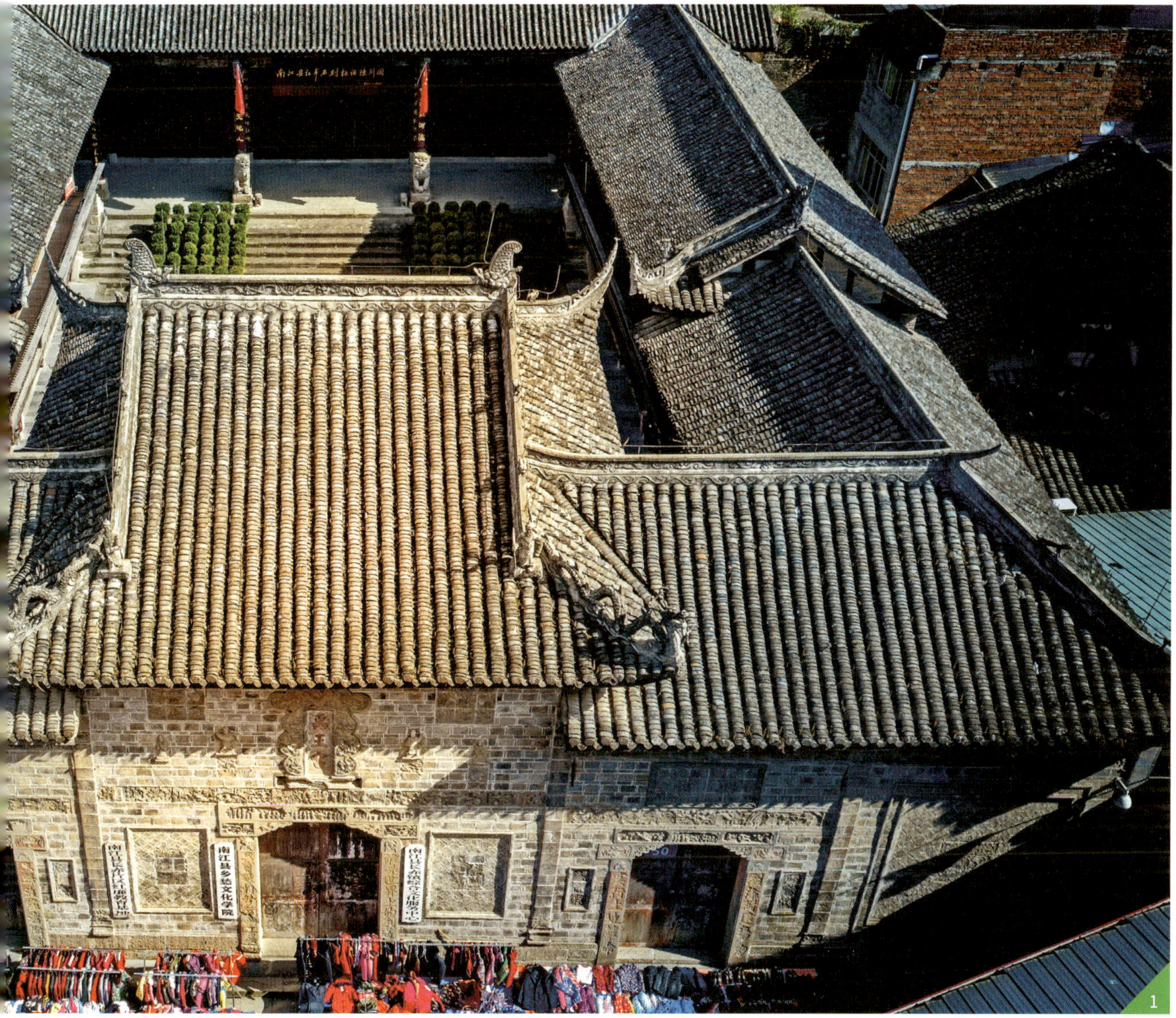

1

3

4

中國工農紅軍

红色剧目《望红台》

《望红台》是巴中市巴州区组织创作的大型舞台曲艺剧。剧长约 85 分钟，以“坚定的信念 守望的情怀”为主题，以川陕苏区为切入点，通过苦水台变成甜水台再变成望红台的历史演绎，表达川陕苏区人民坚定的信念和守望的情怀。

Waiting Terrace for Red Army, a Revolutionary Play

Created by Bazhou District, Bazhong, this play is an 85-minute-long large-scale stage opera on the theme of "firm belief and eager expectation", with the Sichuan-Shaanxi Soviet Area as the starting point, through the historical turning of the bitter into the sweet and then into the terrace for expecting the Red Army by the local people.

左图　成亮 / 摄
红色剧目《望红台》
右上图　夏雨 / 摄
红色剧目《小军号》
右下图　杨继波 / 摄
红色剧目《我的两万个兄弟》

Left Photo / Cheng Liang
***Waiting Terrace for Red Army*, a Revolutionary Play**
Top Right Photo / Xia Yu
***Small Bugle*, a Revolutionary Play**
Bottom Right Photo / Yang Jibo
***My Twenty-Thousand Brothers*, a Revolutionary Play**

张学金 / 摄
"平分土地"红军石刻标语

Photo / Zhang Xuejin
Red Army's Stone Slogan of "Equal Distribution of Land"

平
分

第四章

非物质文化

巴中非物质文化资源内容丰富、风格独特、形式多样，有六大类，具体包含民间文学、传统音乐、传统舞蹈、传统戏剧、曲艺、传统美术、传统技艺、传统医药、民俗和传统体育、游艺及杂技等。现有巴山背二歌、翻山铰子国家级非物质文化遗产项目 2 个，巴中皮影戏等省级非物质文化遗产项目 23 个，有市级和县区级非物质文化遗产项目多项，有国家、省、市、县区级非物质文化遗产传承人 200 余名。建有传承基地、传习所 20 余个，四川省首批非物质文化遗产项目体验基地 10 余个。编印出版了《巴山情歌》等非物质文化遗产题材系列丛书 30 余套。创作的四川清音《中华医药》等非物质文化遗产题材文艺作品先后获全国群星奖等 20 余个国家级奖项、60 余个省级奖项。

张学金 / 摄
巴中皮影戏（省级非物质文化遗产）

Photo / Zhang Xuejin
Bazhong Shadow Play (provincial intangible cultural heritage)

Chapter 4

Intangible Culture

Bazhong intangible cultural resources, rich in content, unique in style and diverse in form, is possessed of 6 categories, including folk literature, traditional music, traditional dance, traditional drama, folk art, traditional fine arts, traditional skills, traditional medicine, folklore and traditional sports, and entertainment and acrobatics. There still exist 2 national-level intangible cultural heritage items (Bashan Porters and Dancing of Fanshanjiazi), 23 provincial-level ones such as Bazhong shadow play, and many more city- and county-level intangible ones, a total of 200-plus inheritors at all levels. There are over 20 inheritance bases and training centers, and 10-odd experience bases for the first intangible cultural heritage items in Sichuan Province. It has edited and published over 30 books series related to this heritage represented by *Bashan Love Songs*. Literary and artistic works like *Chinese Medicine* of Sichuan Qingyin and others have respectively won over 20 and 60 provincial awards represented by National Star Award.

罗元权 / 摄 Photo / Luo Yuanquan
巴山背二歌 **Bashan Porters' Song**

巴山背二歌

巴山背二歌为国家级非物质文化遗产保护项目，产生并流传于川东北，起源于“背二歌”长途背运劳动之中，有3000多年历史，歌词常采用赋、比、兴等手法，多为上下句结构和徵调式，其旋律流畅、节奏自由、声音高亢、风格粗犷，极具地域特色。

Bashan Porters' Song

With a history of more than 3,000 years, Bashan Porters' Song, as a national-level intangible cultural heritage for preservation produced and spread in northeastern Sichuan, originated from the long-distance transportation of porters. Through the use of varied artistic techniques in the lyrics, it carries a strong local feature due to the smooth melody, free rhythm, high-pitched and unconstrained style.

翻山铰子

翻山铰子为国家级非物质文化遗产保护项目，产生并流传于平昌县龙岗镇、西兴镇一带，为汉族民间舞蹈杰出代表，因表演时挥动铰子或甩过头顶、或绕过腰腿形似翻山而得名。该舞蹈起源于傩戏，流传于民间，定型于明清，成熟于民国，分高台铰子、平地铰子、异形铰子等，是研究巴文化的活化石。平昌县龙岗镇为中国民间文化艺术之乡、四川省民间文化艺术之乡。

Dancing of Fanshanjiaozi

Produced and spread around Longgang and Xixing Towns in Pingchang County, Fanshanjiaozi, as a national intangible cultural heritage for preservation, is an outstanding folk dance popular with the Han nationality. Its name comes from the way of the dancers' movement when they wave their Jiaozi (copper cymbals) overhead, round the waist and legs as if climbing the mountain (fanshan). This dancing originated from the popular Nuo Opera, got finalized in the Ming and Qing Dynasties, and matured in the Republic of China. It can be performed on the table, and (even) on the (irregular) ground, hence a living fossil for the study of Ba culture. Pingchang's Longgang Town is home to the provincial and national folk culture and art.

平昌县文广旅局供图
翻山铰子

Photo / Courtesy of Pingchang Bureau of Culture, Radio and Tourism
Dancing of Fanshanjiaozi

正月十六登高

农历正月十六登高，省级非物质文化遗产保护项目，是巴中传统的民俗节日活动，源于巴人正月十六游山走百病的习俗，沿袭至今已有千年历史。其风俗有游山拜庙、礼佛、摸福寿、求子、采小柏桠别在身上或头上去病驱邪等，为研究巴中民俗历史、民俗信仰、民俗文化提供了宝贵的实物资料。

Hill Climbing on 16th of First Month in Chinese Lunar New Year

This traditional folk festival of over 1,000 years in Bazhong, and a provincial intangible cultural heritage for preservation, originates from such customs as visiting temples, paying homage to Buddha, drawing lots for blessing and longevity, begging for sons in caves, and wearing a cypress branch on the person or head against diseases, which provides valuable concrete materials for the study of Bazhong folk history, folk beliefs, and folk culture.

巴中市文化馆供图
正月十六登高（省级非物质文化遗产）

Photo / Courtesy of Bazhong Cultural Center
Hill Climbing on 16th of First Month in Chinese Lunar New Year (provincial intangible cultural heritage)

1 李亚雪作品
四川剪纸(巴山剪纸)(省级非物质文化遗产)
2 李杰供图
龙舞(恩阳尹家飞龙)(省级非物质文化遗产)
3 彭从凯 / 摄
巴山婚俗(市级非物质文化遗产)
4 叶君 / 摄
嚢坛戏(省级非物质文化遗产)
5 张学金 / 摄
说春(省级非物质文化遗产)

1. Paper-Cutting by Li Yaxue
Bashan Paper-Cutting, Sichuan (provincial intangible cultural heritage)
2. Photo / Li Jie
Dragon Dance (Yinjia Town, Enyang) (provincial intangible cultural heritage)
3. Photo / Peng Congkai
Wedding Sedan Chair in Bashan (municipal intangible cultural heritage)
4. Photo / Ye Jun
Cuantan Opera (provincial intangible cultural heritage)
5. Photo / Zhang Xuejin
Spring Singing (provincial intangible cultural heritage)

1

2

3

4

5

第二篇

旅游

Part 2

Tourism

巴中市树 / 巴山水青冈
Bazhong City Tree - Fagus Lucida

第一章

景区旅游

巴中生态环境良好、旅游资源富集，且资源种类多、分布广、禀赋高，全市主要旅游资源涵盖标准 8 大主类的全部类型，涉及 23 个亚类中的 20 个亚类和 110 个基本类型中的 58 个基本类型，主要资源单体有 377 个。巴中有世界地质公园 1 个、国家 AAAAA 级旅游景区 1 个、国家 AAAA 级旅游景区 21 个、国家森林公园 4 个、国家水利风景区 4 个、国家湿地公园 1 个。人间仙境光雾山，重峦叠嶂，气势磅礴，有“山奇、石怪、谷幽、水秀、峰险”五绝，四季景色美轮美奂，是全国生态旅游示范区。神奇诡异诺水河，境内秀水中流、险峰兀立、怪石丛生，地下溶洞密布、洞洞相连、纵横交错、乳笋林立、千姿百态，是游客探险猎奇胜地。空山天盆、临江丽峡、小巫峡、唱歌石林、神门风景等景点，意境绝艳，心随景飞，令人流连忘返。“吃住行游购娱”优质服务，“商养学闲情奇”消费热点，观光体验、旅居康养、研学科考等多样业态，展现了巴中景区旅游的多姿多彩和独特魅力。

肖洪波 / 摄　巴中市文旅集团供图
米仓山旅游景区

Photo / Xiao Hongbo of Bazhong Cultural Tourism Group
Mt. Micang Scenic Area

Chapter 1

Scenic Tourism

Highly bestowed with its good ecological environment, rich and various resources and wide distribution, Bazhong's main tourism resources cover all the 8 major categories, involving 20 of the 23 subcategories and 58 of the 110 basic categories, which totals 377 items of the main resources. It has 1 global geopark, 1 national AAAA-level tourist scenic area, 1 national AAAAA-level tourist scenic area, 21 national AAAA-level tourist scenic area, 4 national forest parks, 4 national water conservancy scenic spots, and 1 national wetland park. Mt. Guangwu, a national demonstration area for eco-tourism, resembles a fairyland on earth, where one grand peak rises higher than another, characterized by its unique hills, grotesque rocks, secluded valleys, clear water and steep cliffs, in addition to its beautiful change of every season.Nuoshui River, magical and exotic, with clean water flowing through, steep peaks, grotesque rocks, dense underground karst caves, and crisscrossed but connected caves, makes an ideal destination for adventurous tourists. So enchanting are such scenic spots as Kongshan Natural Bonsai, Linjiangli Gorge, Xiaowu Gorge, Changge Stone Forest and Shenmen scenery! Its all-round, tourists' experience, residing for healthcare, research and expedition and others are a good showcase of Bazhong's colorful and unique charms.

光雾山旅游区

光雾山旅游区位于巴中市文旅新区，地处中国南北气候分界线、冷暖气候交会处，被称为“南方的北方，北方的南方”，是世界地质公园、国家 AAAAA 级旅游景区、全国生态文明景区、中华秦岭 100 景、四川最美林草景观、四川最受网民喜爱的网红打卡地 TOP100。景区面积 830 平方千米，由光雾山旅游景区、米仓山旅游景区、十八月潭旅游景区、小巫峡景区、神门景区五大景区组成，集秀峰怪石、峭壁幽谷、溪流瀑潭、原始山林为一体，山奇、石怪、谷幽、水秀、峰险为光雾山“五绝”，是国内资源禀赋极高的自然山水原生态景区。景区气候宜人，年均气温 13 °C，负氧离子含量超 3 万个 / 立方厘米，是“春赏山花，夏戏山水，秋品红叶，冬览冰挂”的国内旅游重要目的地。景区森林覆盖率达 97.5%，有野生维管束植物近 2300 种，古植物化石“巴山水青冈”4 万余亩，野生动物有 26 目、61 科、275 种。光雾山红叶具有面积大、气势壮观，色彩丰、五彩斑斓，周期长、景色分明，种类多、内容丰富，品位高、出身名门等特点，观赏时间长达月余，为“新蜀中九绝”，被誉为“亚洲最长红地毯”。旅游区举办光雾山冰雪节、光雾山杜鹃花节、光雾山国际红叶节，推出全国首部大型行浸式山水夜游《梦境光雾山》，是电视剧《远山的红叶》拍摄地。旅游区所在的光雾山镇为全国文明村镇、国家级生态乡镇、天府旅游名镇，光雾山镇焦家河村为国家森林乡村。

Mt. Guangwu Tourist Scenic Area

This scenic area, located in Bazhong Cultural Tourism New Area, is China's north-south climatic divide, or intersection of its cold and warmth. That is why it is called its "north of the south and south of the north". It is not only a global geopark, one of the national AAAAA-level tourist and ecologically-advanced scenic areas, but also of the 100 scenic spots in the Qinling Mountains, Sichuan's most beautiful forest and grass landscape, and one of Sichuan's top 100 Internet celebrity-packed places. It covers an area of over 830 million square meters and is made up of such five parts as Mt. Guangwu, Mt. Micang, Eighteen-Moon Pool, Xaiowu Gorge, and Shenmen, integrating beautiful peaks and strange rocks, cliffs and valleys, streams, waterfalls, and virgin forests. Among them, Mt. Guangwu boasts such qualities as unique shape, grotesque rock, quiet valley and steep peak, hence an ecological scenic spot domestically known for its rich natural resources. The climate here is pleasant, with an average annual temperature of 13°C and negative oxygen ion content of over 30,000 per cubic centimeter, hence a key destination for domestic tourists "to enjoy spring flowers, summer landscape, autumn red leaves and winter icicles". With a forest coverage rate of 97.5%, it possesses about 2,300 species of wild vascular plants, over 40,000 mu of ancient plant fossils of "Bashan fagus lucida", in addition to 275 species of wild animals in 26 orders and 61 families. Mt. Guangwu has a large area of red leaves, magnificent, rich, varied, dignified, which lasts more than a month, hence the name of "the longest red carpet in Asia" and one of Sichuan's nine wonders. As the filming location for the TV series of *Red Leaves in the Distant Mountains*, it has held such festivals as Ice and Snow, Azalea, International Red Leaves, and staged China's first large-scale immersion landscape night tour of *Dreamland of Light and Mist*. Guangwushan, where the scenic spot is located, is a culturally progressive and ecological town at the national level, and one of Sichuan's famous tourist towns, and its Jiaojiahe is a national forest village.

李妮珈 / 摄
光雾山—诺水河地质公园博物馆

Photo / Li Nijia
Mt. Guangwu-Nuoshui River Geopark Museum

光雾山旅游景区

光雾山旅游景区位于巴中市文旅新区，川陕交界处，是光雾山一诺水河世界地质公园地质奇观集中呈现地。“光雾”在方言中表示“都是雾，全是雾”，因常年被雾气笼罩，因而得名光雾山。光雾山山峰气势雄伟，常年云雾缠绕，独特的地理气候和特殊的大地构造背景，造就了奇特的喀斯特岭脊峰丛地貌、古朴的原生态植被和清幽的峡谷风光。景区主要有七女峰、燕岩石林、龙驾烟云、万笏朝圣、太极天坑、飞云栈道等精品景点。

小图　肖洪波 / 摄
栖息在光雾山景区的大鲵
大图　巴中市文旅集团供图
两河口景点

Small Photo / Xiao Hongbo
Andrias Davidianus in Mt. Guangwu
Big Photo / Courtesy of Bazhong Cultural Tourism Group
Lianghekou

Mt. Guangwu Tourist Scenic Area

This scenic area, where Sichuan borders on Shaanxi and located in Bazhong Cultural Tourism New Area, is the place where the geographical wonders gather in the Mt. Guangwu-Nuoshui River Geopark. "Guangwu" means "all fog or fog all around " according to the dialect of locals, hence the name. It has a majestic peak surrounded by clouds and mist all year round owing to the unique geographical climate and special tectonic background, which has created a unique karst ridge and peak cluster, primitive ecological vegetation and quiet canyons. Here there are such key scenic spots as Seven-Fairy Peaks, Yanyan Rock Forest, Dragon-Riding Cloud, Tablet-Holding Courtiers Before the Monarch, Tai Chi Tiankeng, and Feiyun Plank Road.

左图　巴中市文旅集团供图　　Left Photo / Courtesy of Bazhong Cultural Tourism Group

燕子岭云海　　**Sea of Clouds Over Yanziling**

右图　肖洪波 / 摄　　Right Photo / Xiao Hongbo

生活在燕子岭的红白鼯鼠　　**Petaurista Alborufus in Yanziling**

燕岭仙岛景点

光雾山旅游景区燕子岭绝壁下有一个巨大溶洞，数万只燕子、岩雀常年栖息于洞中，成群绕飞于云天石林之上，燕岭由此得名。走上燕岭环线，景随步移，一步一景，南天门、七女峰、万笏朝圣、云天飞燕等景点接踵而至，阳光、云雾、峰丛、山林交相辉映。燕岭仙岛是光雾山十景之一。

Yanling Fairyland

In Mt. Guangwu Tourist Scenic Area there lies a huge karst cave, in which lodge tens of thousands of swallows and rock sparrows all year round, flying in groups above the Yuntian Stone Forest, hence the name of Yanling (Ridge of Swallows). Within a few steps along the Yanling Ring Road, tourists can be greeted by such scenes as Nantianmen (Door to Southern Sky), Qinvfeng (Seven-Fairy Peaks), Tablet-Holding Courtiers Before the Monarch, Yuntian Feiyan (Flying Swallows Overhead) one after another, where the sun, clouds, peaks, mountains and forests set each other off. This fairyland is one of the ten scenic spots in Mt. Guangwu.

巴中市文旅集团供图
燕岭仙岛
Photo / Courtesy of Bazhong Cultural Tourism Group
Yanling Fairyland

七女峰景点

自焦家河畔一道山梁拔地而起，绵延而上燕岩峰，在几十座峰丛中有七座格外引人注目，其宛如仙女，亭亭玉立，俊秀典雅，神韵非凡，云雾飘浮其间，宛若仙境。费孝通曾为七女峰题词“人间仙境光雾山”。七女峰四季景色各异，春天山花飘香，夏季绿树葱茏，深秋彩叶满山，隆冬冰雪压枝。

肖洪波 / 摄
七女峰景点

Photo / Xiao Hongbo
Seven-Fairy Peaks

Seven-Fairy Peaks

From Jiaojia River rises a ridge, stretching all the way up to Yanyan Peak. Of dozens of such peaks, only seven are so eye-catching just like fairies, who are standing erect and elegant above the cloudy fairyland. No wonder Fei Xiaotong, China's contemporary sociologist, inscribed thus, "Mt. Guangwu, Fairyland on Earth". It looks quite varied in four reasons: fragrant flowers in spring, green trees in summer, colorful mountains in autumn, and ice and snow on branches in winter.

万笏朝圣景点

从燕子岭向东前行至观景台上，远眺层峦叠嶂、林海苍茫，近看峰丛林立、千姿百态。对面穿心岭与七女峰遥遥相对，之间峡谷出口较小，里面宽阔，形似葫芦形，因峡谷产有“火链”石头（火石），取名火石塘。在火石塘里，大小峰丛遍布其间，依序绵延至四周，极为壮观，如蜡烛直立、并蒂莲花，似帆船起航，像古人朝靴等，形状各异。左侧有一尊形如巨大人像的石峰端坐于山崖之上，俯视着火石塘四周的群峰石林，形似“万笏朝圣”。

巴中市文旅集团供图
万笏朝圣景点

Photo / Courtesy of Bazhong Cultural Tourism Group
Tablet-Holding Courtiers Before the Monarch

Tablet-Holding Courtiers Before the Monarch

Strolling eastward from Yanzi Ridge to the Viewing Platform, one can see range upon range of wooded mountains in the distance and one peak after another nearby, each in a different pose. Chuanxin Ridge and Seven-Fairy Peaks, though some distance off, stand facing each other. The canyon in between resembles a gourd in that its exit is so narrow and interior so broad. It is called Flint Pond as a producer of flint. All around it, there stand spectacular peaks of every size, stretching in every direction, which look like candles standing upright, twin lotus flowers on one stalk, boats setting sail, or court boots worn by ancients. To the left, there sits a giant stone on the cliff, overlooking all peaks and stone forests surrounding the Pond, hence a scene of "Tablet-Holding Courtiers Before the Monarch".

飞云栈道景点

飞云栈道位于 280 米的绝壁之上，这里绝壁如巨石垒成，当地人称“磊石岩”，其节理裂隙呈水平发育，是光雾山岩溶地质形成的重点区域。人行其间，如凌空行云，飞身踏雾。栈道因势而建，曲折、惊险、刺激。

Feiyun (Flying Cloud) Plank Road

This plank road, located on the 280-meter-high cliff called "Piled-Up Grag" by the locals, seems to be on a pile of huge stones, which develops horizontally. Walkers on it feel as if in the flying clouds. It has just been built as the situation requires, full of twists and turns, thrilling and exciting.

张朝阳 / 摄
飞云栈道景点

Photo / Zhang Chaoyang
Feiyun Plank Road

太极天坑景点

太极天坑是光雾山旅游景区的精品景观。是典型的锅墙地貌，焦家河水将岩溶山体切割成 S 形状，如太极图案，称为“太极天坑”。焦家河流如一条翡翠玉带缠绕于峡谷之间。奇山生奇峰，奇峰俊山河，在群山、峭壁的怀抱中，孕育出珍珠般美丽的绿岛，灌木成荫，绿树葱茏，如蓬莱仙境，似清水芙蓉。一座奇异的绿峰拱立，如情侣重逢、如龙角倚天、如孔雀开屏、如桃园结义。周围悬崖峭壁上的地质奇观，令众多地质学家惊叹不已。斗转星移，岁月沧桑，大自然在不经意间造就出这般美景。

Tai Chi Tiankeng

As a key landscape in Mt. Guangwu Tourist Area, this scenic spot is of typical Guoqiang landform, where Jiaojia River, which winds around the canyon like a jade belt, cuts the karst mountain into an S shape, as if after the Tai Chi pattern, hence the name. Surrounded by mountains and cliffs, there is a green island as beautiful as a pearl, where the shrubs are shady and the trees verdant, like a fairyland in Penglai, or a lotus out of clean water. A strangely-shaped green peak stands like lovers newly-reunited, a dragon's horn touching the sky, or a peacock opening its tail. The geological wonders on the surrounding cliffs have amazed many geologists. All this has been created by nature accidentally with the passage of time.

上图 巴中市兰花协会供图
线叶春兰素花
下图 巴中市文旅集团供图
太极天坑景点

Above Photo / Courtesy of Bazhong Orchid Association
C. Georingii Var. Serratum
Below Photo / Courtesy of Bazhong Cultural Tourism Group
Tai Chi Tiankeng

云天飞燕景点

Yuntian Feiyan (Flying Swallows Overhead)

巴中市文旅新区供图
Photo / Courtesy of Bazhong Cultural Tourism New Area

龙驾烟云景点

龙架山自焦家河畔拔地而起，横卧绿水蓝天之间，常被一层或浓或淡的云雾缠绕，若隐若现，取名“龙驾烟云”。龙架山形如巨龙骨架，分为上中下三层，上层高低错落。大小山峰犹如龙的脊骨，中层绵延林木如龙身，下层大小十八座山峰如龙须和龙爪。龙架山雨后天晴的早晨，山顶会出现红云罩山顶的奇观，山间云雾缥缈，青山若隐若现，神奇壮观。

Cloud-Riding Dragon

Mt. Longjia, which rises above Jiaojia River, lies between the clear water and azure sky, and is usually surrounded by a layer of clouds either thick or thin, hence the name of "Cloud-Riding Dragon". It is shaped like a giant dragon skeleton of three layers: the upper one, so well-proportioned, with large peaks as its spine; the middle one, of continuous forests as its body, and the lower one, of 18 large and small peaks as its beards and claws. On the sunny morning after the rain, a spectacle of red clouds will present itself above its top, so mysterious with mist afloat below and green hills partly hidden and partly visible.

巴中市文旅集团供图
龙架山景观

Photo / Courtesy of Bazhong Cultural Tourism Group
Mt. Longjia

上图　巴中市文旅集团供图
天然画廊景点
下图　肖洪波 / 摄
生活在米仓山的黄喉貂

Above Photo / Courtesy of Bazhong Cultural Tourism Group
Natural Gallery
Below Photo / Xiao Hongbo
Martes Flavigula in Mt. Micang

米仓山旅游景区

米仓山旅游景区位于巴中市文旅新区，是光雾山旅游区的重要组成部分，是四川米仓山国家森林公园所在地，以红叶观赏闻名于世，有“亚洲最长红地毯”“中国红叶之乡”等美誉。景区森林覆盖率97.3%，负氧离子含量超 3 万个 / 立方厘米，国家一级、二级保护动植物多达数十种，是名副其实的“秦巴山区生物基因库”。这里四季皆景，春有山花烂漫，姹紫嫣红；夏有绿海葱茏，林冠翻波；秋有巴山红叶，层林尽染；冬有林海雪原，玉树琼花。景区地质地貌奇特，其山秀如峨眉，林幽似青城。景区主要有贾郭山、天然画廊、黑熊沟、香炉山、大小兰沟、牟阳故城、巴山温带珍稀植物园等精品景点。

Mt. Micang Tourist Scenic Area

Located in the Bazhong Cultural Tourism New Area and as a key part of Mt. Guangwu Tourist Area, it is the location of Mt. Micang National Forest Park, so well-known as "home to red leaves" and "the longest red carpet in Asia". Its rate of forest coverage is 97.3%, content of negative oxygen ions over 30,000 per cubic centimeter, and dozens of species of animals and plants under national first and second-level key protection, a veritable "Biological Gene Bank of the Qinling-Bashan Mountains". It is beauty itself here in all seasons for tourists, namely, flowers in spring, luxuriant trees all about in summer, red leaves in autumn and icicles in winter. The peculiar geology and landform here remind one of both Mt. Emei, and Mt. Qingcheng. Its main scenic spots include Mt. Jiaguo, Natural Gallery, Black Bear Gully, Mt. Xianglu, Langou Gully, Mouyang Ancient City, and Bashan Temperate Rare Botanical Garden.

巴中市文旅集团供图
天然画廊景点

Photo / Courtesy of Bazhong Cultural Tourism Group
Natural Gallery

Natural Gallery

It is located in the core area of Mt. Micang Scenic Area as Mt. Guangwu's most distinctive and representative scenery and one of its ten scenic spots. Here, Bashan fagus lucida presents itself so colorfully in all seasons as a poetic picture: in spring, green buds among the treetops together with singing birds show the recovery and vitality of all things; in summer, the lush trees are deep and leafy forest help tourists enjoy the cool to the full; in autumn, the nightly wind in Bashan reddens the leaves as if spring were on the way; and in winter, snow glistens all around with rime and ice, so transparent, hanging on the trees.

天然画廊景点

天然画廊景点位于米仓山旅游景区核心地带，是光雾山最有特色、最具代表性的景点，是光雾山十景之一。巴山水青冈五彩斑斓彩林呈现，四季皆美，如诗如画。春天，绿芽在树梢间萌动，飞鸟在丛林中啼鸣，万物复苏勃勃生机；夏天，绿树葱郁，林深叶茂，穿行其间，暑气顿消；秋天，巴山一夜风，木叶映天红，色比桃花艳，秋如春意浓；冬天，玉树琼花，银装素裹，雾凇冰挂，玲珑剔透。

大小兰沟景点

大小兰沟景点位于米仓山旅游景区，山水与林木交融，红叶与碧潭辉映，是光雾山品鉴红叶的最佳之地。漫步红叶林中，观千山万壑染尽，赏溪流瀑潭浸透，品不完的红叶风韵，享不尽的诗情画意。兰沟醉红是光雾山十景之一。

左图　右图　巴中市文旅新区供图
大小兰沟景点

Left and Right Photos Courtesy of Bazhong Cultural Tourism New Area
Langou Gully

Langou Gully

Located in Mt. Micang Tourist Area, where mountains and rivers blend with forests, and red leaves and blue pools reflect each other, it makes the best place to appreciate red leaves across Mt. Guangwu. You can just walk in the red-leaf forest, watching the mountain and valley thus dyed, viewing streams, waterfalls and pools, feasting your eyes on the endless charming leaves, and enjoying whatever so poetic and picturesque. Langou Gully is one of the ten scenic spots in Mt. Guangwu.

黑熊沟景点

Black Bear Gully

巴中市文旅集团供图
Photo / Courtesy of Bazhong Cultural Tourism Group

大象迎宾景点

Guest-Greeting Elephant

巴中市文旅集团供图
Photo / Courtesy of Bazhong Cultural Tourism Group

牟阳星空景点

Starry Sky Over Mouyang

巴中市文旅集团供图
Photo / Courtesy of Bazhong Cultural Tourism Group

贾郭山景点

贾郭山景点位于米仓山旅游景区，属典型的岭脊型喀斯特峰丛地貌，几十座山峰一字并列排开，错落有致，如群龙列阵，威风凛凛，昂首挺立，似欲出云海试比高。山下林海茫茫，无尽的小山岭依附着主峰顺势排列，蜿蜒曲折，常有云雾翻腾，或缠绕群峰，或填埋沟壑。春日山花争艳，生机盎然；夏季林海茫茫，无边无际；秋天七彩织锦，如梦如幻；寒冬林海雪原，玉碾乾坤。贾郭丛峰是光雾山十景之一。

Mt. Jiaguo

Located in Mt. Micang Tourist Scenic Area as one of its ten scenic spots, it enjoys a typical ridge-type karst peak cluster landform with dozens of peaks lined up side by side in a well-arranged pattern, like a group of dragons, majestic and upright, as if trying to vie for height with the sea of clouds. A vast sea of forest at its foot and endless hills are placed round the main peak, winding and sinuous, often with clouds and mist around; in spring, all the hills and flowers contend in beauty and are full of vitality; in summer, the sea of forest appears boundless; in autumn, all the colors make a brocade of a dream; and in winter, the snow-clad forest is so white as a vast jade. Mt Jiaguo is one of the ten scenic spots in Mt. Guangwu.

巴中市文旅集团供图
贾郭丛峰景点

Photo / Courtesy of Bazhong Cultural Tourism Group
Mt. Jiaguo

香炉山索道

Cableway in Mt. Xianglu

巴中市文旅集团供图
Photo / Courtesy of Bazhong Cultural Tourism Group

大坝景区路

Dam Scenic Road

上图 胡鹏 / 摄
下图 张小东 / 摄

Above Photo / Hu Peng
Below Photo / Zhang Xiaodong

上图　巴中市文旅集团供图
香炉日出
下左图　巴中市文旅集团供图
香炉云海
下右图　肖洪波 / 摄
生活在香炉山的红腹角雉

Above Photo / Courtesy of Bazhong Cultural Tourism Group
Sunrise over Mt. Xianglu
Below Left Photo / Courtesy of Bazhong Cultural Tourism Group
Sea of Clouds over Mt. Xianglu
Below Right Photo / Xiao Hongbo
Chrysolophus Pictus in Eighteen-Moon Pool

香炉山景点

香炉山景点位于米仓山旅游景区，四道龙脊山岭向四周延伸，远望酷似一个巨型香炉而得名，海拔 2330 米，为米仓山旅游景区第一高峰。这里日出和云海相生相伴，黎明时分，太阳从云海中喷薄而出，越过山脊，照亮大地，一切等待化为感动，万千忧愁随之飘散。日上三竿，杜鹃、崖柏、云海、雾凇等香炉四绝画卷，跟随季节的变化渐次展开，使人身心舒展在群峰耸峙的崇岭之巅。香炉日出是光雾山十景之一。

Mt. Xianglu （Incense Burner）

Located in Mt. Micang Tourist Scenic Area, with its four ridges extending far, it looks like a giant incense burner when viewed in the distance, hence the name. It is 2,330 meters above sea level, the highest peak of the area. The sun here, always accompanied by a sea of clouds, rises over it, crosses the ridges, and illuminates the earth. All who wait for and see that sight will be greatly moved and their sorrow gone in no time. In the sun, the four masterpieces of azalea, cypress, cloud sea, and rime display their beauty in turn with the change of seasons, making everyone present stretch themselves, both physically and mentally. It is one of the ten scenic spots in Mt. Guangwu.

大坝雾凇景点

大坝雾凇是光雾山十景之一。每逢寒冬来临，空气中无数在 0 °C以下而尚未凝结的大量水蒸气，随风在树枝上不断积聚冻结，形成非冰非雪的雾凇奇观。光雾山雾凇品质之佳、形态之奇、面积之大，国内罕见。独特冬景，不是北国，胜似北国。欲观雾凇之奇，唯大坝莫属。若于天朗气清之日，蓝天白云之下，以“仙境”概论尚显不足。

大图　小图　巴中市文旅集团供图
大坝雾凇

Photos Courtesy of Bazhong Cultural Tourism Group
Dam Rime

Dam Rime

It is one of the ten scenic spots in Mt. Guangwu. Whenever winter comes, there is plenty of sub-zero yet uncondensed water vapor in the air which, in the wake of wind, keeps accumulating on the branches, hence a spectacle of rime that is neither ice nor snow. The rime here is rare across China in terms of quality, shape and extent. This unique winter scene makes visitors unsure whether or not they are still in South China. For such a wonder, there is no better place. In case of fresh air with white clouds in the azure sky, people will find themselves in a true fairyland.

大图　张学金 / 摄
香炉山云岭花海景点
小图　巴中市文旅集团供图
香炉山杜鹃

Big Photo / Zhang Xuejin
Yunling Sea of Flowers at Mt. Xianglu
Small Photo / Courtesy of Bazhong Cultural Tourism Group
Azalea Across Mt. Xianglu

香炉山杜鹃

春赏杜鹃是光雾山春季旅游的特色，而香炉山的高山杜鹃则是这一特色中的极品。每年 5 月，香炉山的云雾与绽放的高山杜鹃如期相约，云岭花海景象便展露无遗。绽放在云蒸雾绕的山岭上的杜鹃花，或傲然而立，或绝壁丛生，或纯真素雅，或娇艳欲滴，争奇斗艳地汇集成一片花的海洋。云岭花海是光雾山十景之一。

Azalea Across Mt. Xianglu

Admiring azalea is a feature of spring tourism in Mt. Guangwu, where the alpine azalea is at its prime. In May every year, the clouds and mist over Mt. Xianglu meet it as usual, and the sea of flowers is fully revealed. The azalea , in full bloom and surrounded by clouds and mist, stands proudly, or in clusters on cliffs, or looks pure and elegant, or charming, all blended into a sea of flowers. Yunling Sea of Flowers is one of the ten scenic spots of Mt. Guangwu.

十八月潭旅游景区

十八月潭旅游景区位于巴中市文旅新区，是光雾山旅游区的重要组成部分，主峰海拔 2508 米，是川东北第一高峰。景区主要由十八月潭、九角山、玉印台等精品景点组成。其间森林茂密、瀑潭众多，密布着 18 个恍若神造仙成的瀑潭，潭形似月桂，以花岗石为底，古木镶边，瀑潭相连，一步一景，令人心旷神怡，被称为“川东北的九寨沟”。一入秋，层林尽染，万山红遍，素有“月潭赛九寨，红叶天下绝”的美誉。

Eighteen-Moon Pool

Located in Bazhong Cultural Tourism New Area, it is a key part of Mt. Guangwu Tourist Area, its main peak being 2508 meters above sea level, the highest in Northeastern Sichuan. This densely-covered forest is dotted with 18 ingenious waterfalls and pools. Each of these pools is shaped like a moon, with granite at the bottom and ancient trees around, and closely linked, which makes one scene another, refreshing tourists as they walk and halt. Little wonder it is called "Jiuzhaigou in Northeastern Sichuan". Once autumn approaches all the wooded mountains are dyed red, hence the repute of "All moon pools match Jiuzhai, and red leaves fill the sky".

大图　张学金 / 摄
十八月潭景区
小图　肖洪波 / 摄
生活在十八月潭的红腹锦鸡

Big Photo / Zhang Xuejin
Eighteen-Moon Pool
Small Photo / Xiao Hongbo
Chrysolophus Pictus in Eighteen-Moon Pool

1 巴中市文旅集团供图
情侣潭
2 巴中市文旅集团供图
婚纱瀑布
3 巴中市文旅集团供图
云梯潭
4 巴中市文旅集团供图
龙潭瀑
5 巴中市文旅集团供图
珍珠潭
6 巴中市文旅集团供图
孔雀潭
7 巴中市文旅集团供图
仙女潭
8 张学金 / 摄
赵公潭

4

6

1.Photo / Courtesy of Bazhong Cultural Tourism Group
Lovers' Pool
2.Photo / Courtesy of Bazhong Cultural Tourism Group
Wedding-Dress Waterfall
3.Photo / Courtesy of Bazhong Cultural Tourism Group
Aerial-Ladder Pool
4.Photo / Courtesy of Bazhong Cultural Tourism Group
Dragon-Pool Waterfall
5.Photo / Courtesy of Bazhong Cultural Tourism Group
Pearl Pool
6.Photo / Courtesy of Bazhong Cultural Tourism Group
Peacock Pool
7.Photo / Courtesy of Bazhong Cultural Tourism Group
Fairy Pool
8.Photo / Zhang Xuejin
Lord Zhao Pool

7

5

8

九角山景点

Mt. Jiujiao

巴中市文旅集团供图
Photo / Courtesy of Bazhong Cultural Tourism Group

小巫峡景区

小巫峡景区位于南江县北部，是光雾山旅游区的重要组成部分，主要以溶洞、峡谷、奇石等为景观特色，有五彩洞、穿花洞、奇石苑等精品景点。

上图　丁伟 / 摄
小巫峡猕猴群
下图　巴中市文旅集团供图
小巫峡大佛景点
右图　杨安文 / 摄
小巫峡石门景点

Above Photo / Ding Wei
Macaque Host in Xiaowu Gorge
Below Photo / Courtesy of Bazhong Cultural Tourism Group
Giant Buddha in Xiaowu Gorge
Right Photo / Yang Anwen
Stone Gate at Xiaowu Gorge

Xiaowu Gorge

Located in the north of Nanjiang, it is a key part of Mt. Guangwu Tourist Area, with such key spots as Five-Color Cave, Twisting Cave, and Strange Stone Garden on account of its karst caves, canyons, and strange stones.

董福良供图
神门洞景点

Photo / Dong Fuliang
Shenmen Cave

神门景区

神门景区位于巴中市文旅新区神门乡和贵民镇，是光雾山旅游区的重要组成部分，主要以峰丛、峡谷、石林、溶洞、秀水、林海为景观特色，有神门洞、黄金峡、懒蛇梁等精品景点。

Shenmen Cave

As an important part of Mt. Guangwu Tourist Area, it is located in Bazhong's Shenmen Town and Guimen Township, Cultural Tourism New Area, mainly characterized by peak clusters, canyons, stone forests, karst caves, clean water, and seas of forest. Its scenic spots contain Shenmen Cave, Golden Gorge, and Lazy Snake Ridge.

左图　董福良供图
神门峰丛景点
右图　董福良供图
神门洞一线天景点

Left Photo / Dong Fuliang
Peaks in Shenmen
Right Photo / Dong Fuliang
Line of Sky Along Shenmen Cave

诺水洞天景区

诺水洞天景区位于巴中市文旅新区诺水河镇，为国家AAAA级旅游景区、国家重点风景名胜区，是光雾山一诺水河世界地质公园的重要组成部分。景区面积约221平方千米，景区内峡谷幽深、奇峰突兀、秀水中流、风景秀丽，自南向北分布有九个院子温泉民宿酒店、金童山山地公园、玉皇坝花海、别有洞天溶洞群、十里峡谷漂流等观赏景点和体验项目。这里有世界上发育母岩地质时代最多的溶洞群，已初步探明溶洞128个，被誉为“世界溶洞博览园、中国溶洞博物馆”，洞内可游览面积约20万平方米，阡陌纵横，鬼斧神工；探明洞道长达20千米以上，洞洞相连、洞中有洞。洞内温度常年恒定在18 °C，湿度96%～98%，形成了北纬32 °线上独特的溶洞气候。景区所在的诺水河镇为国家级生态乡镇。

李江 / 摄
蓬莱仙境景观（龙湖洞）

Photo / Li Jiang
Penglai Fairyland

Nuoshui Unique Cave Group

Located in Bazhong's Nuoshuihe Town, Cultural Tourism New Area, it is a AAAA-level tourist scenic area and key scenic spot, both at the national level and a key part of Mt. Guangwu-Nuoshui River World Geopark as well. In this area of about 221 square kilometers, there are deep canyons, abrupt peaks and flowing water. From south to north, there are 9 courtyard homestay hotels with hot springs, Mt. Golden Boy Park, Yuhuangba Flower Sea, and Unique Karst Cave Group, and Ten-Mile Canyon Rafting to be experienced. It contains the largest group of karst caves since the geological time of matrix development and 128 caves have already been preliminarily proven, hence the names of "World Karst Cave Expo Park" and "China's Karst Cave Museum". With a touring area of about 200,000 square meters, the cave is extraordinary workmanship of nature. The cave group has been proven to be over 20 kilometers in length and connected with each other. The temperature in there stays constant at 18°C all year round, and the humidity 96%-98%, forming a unique karst cave climate at the 32nd parallel north latitude. Nuoshuihe, where the scenic spot is located, is a national-level ecological town.

中峰洞

中峰洞又名佛光洞，被称为“地下岩溶博物馆”。分上中下三层、12大景区、36条支洞、72重迷宫、108般奇景，总长15000米。洞中景色集“雄、险、奇、幽、深”于一体，且洞中有洞，洞洞相连，洞洞有景，堪称“天下第一洞”。

Zhongfeng Cave

This cave of 15,000 meters in length, also known as Foguang Cave and much like an "Underground Karst Museum", is made up of upper, middle and lower layers, containing 12 major scenic spots, 36 branch holes, 72 mazes, and 108 wonders. It can be called "the first cave in the world" owing to its "majestic, dangerous, strange, secluded and deep" features, all connected but with different scenes.

杜卫东 / 摄
如意吉祥景观（中峰洞）

Photo / Du Weidong
Best Wish for All (Zhongfeng Cave)

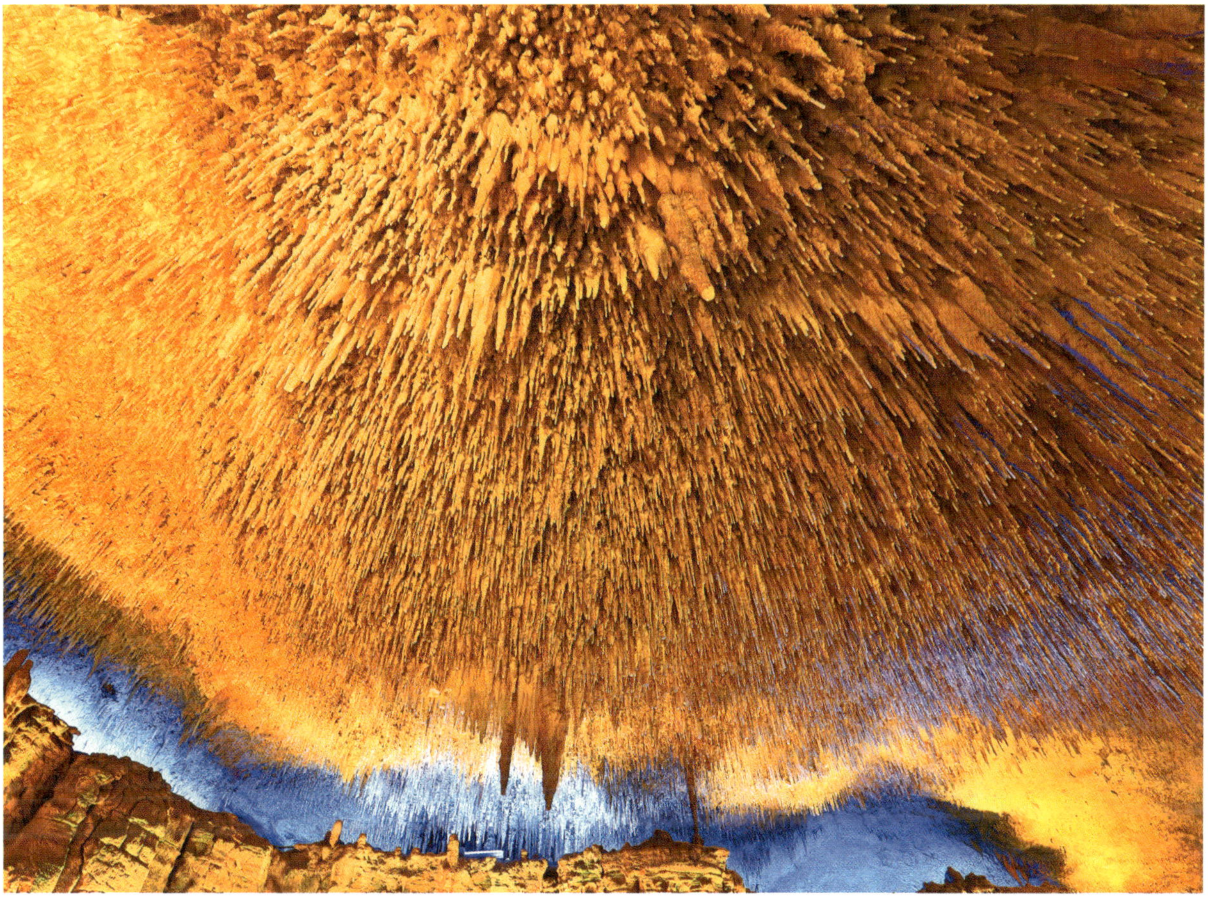

龙湖洞

龙湖洞位于牛角嵌内，可游览面积 5000 万平方米，洞道总长 2000 余米，分上下两层，每层有景点奇观。洞上有洞，洞下有河，河上有湖，如蛟龙盘旋，似水府迷宫。

Longhu Cave

Longhu Cave, located inside Niujiaoqian, with a touring area of 50 million square meters and a total length of over 2,000 meters, is divided into upper and lower layers, each having its scenic spots and wonders. There are caves above each other, rivers under each other, and even lakes above the rivers, like crouching dragons and mazes of water palaces.

左图　何鹏远 / 摄
九莲宝塔景观（龙湖洞）
右图　张学金 / 摄
亿万鹅管景观（龙湖洞）

Left Photo / He Pengyuan
Nine-Lotus Pagoda (**Longhu Cave**)
Right Photo / Zhang Xuejin
Gravitational Water Deposits (**Longhu Cave**)

狮子洞

狮子洞位于牛角嵌北，可游览面积 7000 万平方米。由三殿七庭和“洞中西海”“洞中栈道”等 12 大景观组成，主洞长 2000 余米，高 30 ～ 80 米。洞内塔柱林立，阴河幽邃，四壁乳石满布、形状神奇、气势宏伟。其中，“乳石莲花”“定海神针”“珍珠玉盘”“金龟戏水”和古水文献遗迹堪称绝景。

巴中市文旅集团供图
宝莲台灯景观（狮子洞）

Photo / Courtesy of Bazhong Cultural Tourism Group
Baolian Lamp (Lion Cave)

Lion Cave

Located in the north of Niujiaoqian, with a touring area of 70 million square meters, this cave consists of 12 landscapes (Three Halls plus Seven Courts, West Sea and Plank Road), the main part being over 2,000 meters long and 30-80 meters high. There are numerous towers and columns in the cave, the underground river secluded, the walls covered with galaliths, the shape magical and magnificent. Among them, the "Stalactite Lotus", "Ocean-Quieting Needle", "Pearl Jade Plate", "Golden Turtle Playing in the Water" and the remains of ancient water documents are all superb scenes.

黄龙洞

黄龙洞全长2000余米，可供游览面积达8万平方米以上，由高层化石洞穴和地下河洞穴构成，分上、中、下三层。洞内瀑布、石幔、石幕、石旗、鹅管、石钟乳、石笋、石柱遍布，其中水母石、马牙石、发光的方解石、凸出的燧石、水下晶花、流石坝最具特色，洞内黄龙瀑布宏伟壮观，堪称“诺水一绝”。

Huanglong Cave

With a total length of more than 2,000 meters, and touring area of more than 80,000 square meters, it is composed of high-rise and underground river caves, which are divided into upper, middle and lower layers. There are waterfalls, stone mantles, stone curtains, stone flags, balanophyllia, stalactites, and stone pillars in the cave, among which jellyfish stone, horse tooth stone, luminous calcite, protruding flint, underwater crystal flowers and flow stone dam are the most beautiful. Of the waterfalls inside, Huanglong are the most spectacular.

何嗣猛 / 摄
黄龙瀑布景观（黄龙洞）

Photo / He Simeng
Waterfall (Huanglong Cave)

左图　张学金 / 摄
牛角嵌景观

右上图　巴中市文旅集团供图
别有洞天

右下图　巴中市文旅集团供图
诺水洞漂流

Left Photo / Zhang Xuejin

Landscape at Niujiaoqian

Top Right Photo / Courtesy of Bazhong Cultural Tourism Group

Unique Cave

Below Right Photo / Courtesy of Bazhong Cultural Tourism Group

Rafting down Nuoshui River

玉皇坝景点

玉皇坝景点位于巴中市文旅新区诺水河镇，是诺水洞天景区的组成部分，为一处小型冲积平原，至今仍保留传统农耕文明。这里群山环抱，小溪潺潺，是名副其实的世外桃源。白墙青瓦的民居点缀其间，青山绿水包围中的小村庄是一片净土。

巴中市文旅集团供图
玉皇坝景点

Photo / Bazhong Cultural Tourism Group
Yuhuangba

Yuhuangba

Located in Bazhong's Nuoshuihe Town, Cultural Tourism New Area as an integral part of Nuoshui Unique Cave Group, it is a small alluvial plain which still retains the traditional farming civilization. Surrounded by mountains and gurgling streams, it is a veritable pure paradise, dotted with white house walls and green tiles.

金童山景点

金童山亦称“金童玉女”，位于巴中市文旅新区诺水河镇，山顶双峰相依，形如金童玉女，卓然玉立。上有真武祠，分前、后、楼三殿。登金童山观日出，看夕阳、群山起伏、云海翻腾，听晨钟暮鼓，一派胜景。

Mt. Golden Boy (and Jade Girl)

In Nuoshuihe Town, Bazhong Cultural and Tourist New Area, there stand two graceful peaks alongside on Mt. Jintong (and Yvnv) as if a pair of golden boy and jade girl, hence the name. On this mountain, there is a temple called Zhenwu, which is divided into three halls: front, rear and upper floor. Here it is gratifying to watch the rise and set of the sun, the undulating mountains, the writhing sea of clouds, and listen to the morning bell and evening drum.

左图　易航 / 摄
金童山景点
右图　巴中市文旅新区供图
国画屏景点

Left Photo / Yi Hang
Mt. Golden Boy
Right Photo / Courtesy of Bazhong Cultural Tourism Group
Chinese Painting Scroll

临江丽峡景点

临江丽峡景区位于诺水洞天景区东部，面积约 120 平方千米，有景点 60 余处，是联结诺水洞天景区与空山天盆景区的纽带和走廊。峡谷两岸陡壁如削，峡底河流奔涌，形成飞瀑数十处。峡中观景平台上带一线天，底下一线水。峡区古藤缠树，林茂似海，四季常青。

Linjiang Gorge

Located east of the Nuoshui Unique Cave Group, with an area of about 120 square kilometers and more than 60 scenic spots, it is the link and corridor of Nuoshui Unique Cave Group and Mt. Kongshan Natural Bonsai Areas. The steep walls on both sides seem cut thus, and the river under rushes on, forming a dozen waterfalls. Viewed from the gorge platform, either the sky or the river seems but a line. Here the ancient vines are wrapped around the trees, and the forest is like a sea, evergreen all year round.

右图　王立新 / 摄
临江丽峡瀑布
左图　王立新 / 摄
临江丽峡峡谷

Right Photo / Wang Lixin
Waterfall in Linjiang Gorge
Left Photo / Wang Lixin
Valley Along Linjiang Gorge

空山天盆风景区

空山天盆风景区位于巴中市文旅新区空山镇，地处秦巴山区高山盆地，森林覆盖率达 96% 以上，夏季平均气温 20.6 ℃，是国家森林公园、国家 AAAA 级旅游景区、全国森林康养基地试点建设单位、四川省森林康养基地、四川省首批国家级森林氧吧、四川省最佳森林康养目的地、四川 100 个最美观景拍摄点、“全省 63 个自驾游目的地”之一。景区喀斯特地貌、原始森林与红色遗迹融为一体，有山峰 137 座，挂宝岩、五佛观榜、插旗山、七星灯、森林竹海、千年古树待皇树、空山战役遗址、将军树、红军战壕、红军洞、空山军事会议遗址等景点，是川东北地区集生态观光、避暑度假、启迪寓教、登山探秘于一体的旅游景区。景区所在地空山镇为省生态旅游百佳乡、国家生态乡镇、国家卫生乡镇、全国最美森林小镇，空山镇龙池村为国家森林乡村、中坝村为全国文明村镇。

小图　肖裕孟 / 摄
空山待皇树
大图　李仕亮 / 摄
空山天盆景区

Small Photo / Xiao Yumeng
Emperor-Puzzling Tree at Mt. Kongshan
Big Photo / Li Shiliang
Mt. Kongshan Natural Bonsai Area

Kongshan Natural Bonsai Scenic Area

This area, located in Bazhong's Kongshan Town, Cultural Tourism New Area and the alpine basin of the Qinling-Bashan Mountains, enjoys a forest coverage rate of over 96% and an average summer temperature of 20.6°C. It is a national forest park, AAAA-level tourist scenic area, a pilot construction unit of a national and provincial base for healthcare, one of the first national forest oxygen bars, best forest healthcare destination in Sichuan, one of the provincial 100 most beautiful places, and one of Sichuan's 63 self-driving travel destinations. This area, with 137 peaks and a unity of karst landform, virgin forest and revolutionary relics, embraces famous scenic spots such as Gem-Hanging Crag and Five Tablet-Watching Buddhas, Flag-Planted Mountain, Seven-Star Lantern, Bamboo Sea, 1,000-year-long Emperor-Puzzling Tree, Kongshan Battle Site, General's Tree, Red Army Trench, Red Army Cave, and Kongshan Military Conference Site, which are all tourist attractions in Northeastern Sichuan that integrate ecological sightseeing, summer vacation, enlightenment and education, and mountaineering and exploration. Kongshan, to which this area belongs, is one of the top 100 provincial eco-tourism townships, a national ecological, sanitary and most beautiful forest town, and its Longchi is a national forest village, and Zhongba a national model village.

巴中市文旅新区供图
空山牧歌

Photo / Courtesy of Bazhong Cultural Tourism New Area
Pastoral Song on Mt. Kongshan

1. 肖裕孟 / 摄
七星背剑景点
2. 肖裕孟 / 摄
狮象把水口
3. 肖裕孟 / 摄
空山瀑布
4. 蹇代明 / 摄
空山雪景

1. Photo / Xiao Yumeng
Seven-Star Sword
2. Photo / Xiao Yumeng
Water-Controlling of Lion and Elephant
3. Photo / Xiao Yumeng
Waterfall at Mt. Kongshan
4. Photo / Jian Daiming
Snow-Clad Mt. Kongshan

4

云顶茶乡旅游景区

云顶茶乡旅游景区位于南江县南部，面积 5200 万平方米，是国家 AAAA 级旅游景区、四川省森林康养基地、四川十大最美茶乡。景区生态环境良好，立体气候明显，空气清新，负氧离子含量高，田园风光旖旎，自然风光优美，有自然山水景观、地貌景观、水体景观、天象景观、人文景观、田园风光和生态农业体验等多种景观类型，有云顶仙山、奇险南天门、美丽白鹤嘴、神奇仙人洞等 70 余处景点。云顶茶乡的土壤富含硒元素，是国内重要富硒地带之一，也是四川优质富硒绿茶生产示范基地，所产大叶茶为全国优良品种，“云顶茗兰”“云顶绿芽”牌茶叶多次获国际、国内大奖。云顶茶乡先后举办 7 届“巴中云顶”茶文化旅游节。

Yunding Tea Farm

This scenic area, located in the south of Nanjiang County, with an area of 52 million square meters, is a national AAAA-level one, a base for forest healthcare and one of the top ten tea farms in Sichuan. With its good ecological environment, clear-cut vertical climate, fresh air, high content of negative oxygen ions, and natural scenery, it contains 70-plus scenic spots such as Yunding Fairy Mountain, steep Nantianmen, beautiful Baihezui (White Crane's Beak), and magical Celestial Cave. Yunding Tea Farm, with its soil rich in selenium, is one of China's key selenium-rich areas and a demonstration base for the production of high-quality selenium-rich green tea in Sichuan. Its various brands of quality tea have won many international and domestic awards. This very place has witnessed seven festivals named "Bazhong Yunding" Tea Culture Tourism.

周江 / 摄
云顶茶乡有机茶园

Photo / Zhou Jiang
Organic Tea at Yunding Tea Farm

三十二梁旅游景区

三十二梁旅游景区位于平昌县云台镇和青凤镇，面积 2550 万平方米，是国家 AAAA 级旅游景区、中国美丽休闲乡村、四川省森林康养基地、四川省第二批省级乡村旅游重点村。景区有大小山峰 32 座，有千佛殿、马垭风情小镇、龙井芍药花海、七彩林、樱花长廊、龙尾茶文化产业园、刘家大院、蔡家大院、巴山农耕文化陈列馆等景点，是集生态茶园景观、巴人古村院落和森林康养产业于一体的乡村旅游特色景区。

顾志平 / 摄
三十二梁有机茶园

Photo / Gu Zhiping
Organic Tea Across Thirty-Two Peaks

Thirty-Two Peaks

This scenic spot, located in Pingchang's Yuntai and Qingfeng Towns with an area of 25.5 million square meters, a national AAAA level tourist scenic area and a key village for rural tourism. There are 32 large and small peaks here, including Thousand-Buddha Hall, Maya style town, Longjing peony flower sea, colorful forest, cherry blossom corridor, Longwei Tea Cultural Industrial Park, Courtyards by Liu and Cai Families, and Exhibition Hall for Bashan Farming Culture , which are for characteristic rural tourism integrating ecological tea garden landscape, ancient Ba-style village courtyard and forest healthcare industry.

第二章

红色旅游

巴中红色旅游资源丰富，处在全国 12 个“重点红色旅游区”中的“川陕渝红色旅游区”、全国 30 条“红色旅游精品线路”中。4 个红色景区为全国 100 个“红色旅游经典景区”，6 个红色景区景点为“建党百年红色旅游百条精品线路”之“奇兵入川 · 铁血丹心”精品线路上的重要一环，6 个红色景区为全省重点发展红色旅游经典景区；13 个单位为四川省首批中小学红色教育研学实践基地，6 个单位为四川省青少年社会实践教育基地；3 条航线为首批国家红色旅游精品航线，建成通车全国首条红色主题高速公路——镇（巴）广（安）高速王（坪）至通（江）段；6 个国家 AAAA 级旅游景区以红色旅游资源为支撑，推出 5 条“川陕苏区行 · 从心再出发”等红色旅游精品线路、13 条研学旅行线路，建成 41 个特色研学旅行基地、营地，开发“走红军路、吃红军饭、穿红军衣、看红军剧、唱红军歌、游红军城”系列精品线路和文旅品牌。

何嗣猛 / 摄
红军入川第一镇雕塑

Photo / He Simeng
Sculpture of Sichuan's First Town Red Army Entered

Chapter 2

Red Tourism

Bazhong, rich in red tourism resources, is located in the "Sichuan-Shaanxi-Chongqing Red Tourism Area" among the 12 "Key Red Tourism Areas" and 30 "China's Major Red Tourism Routes". 4 of its red scenic spots are among China's 100, and 6 are a key part of the major route of "Surprise Soldiers into Sichuan · Heroes in War-Torn Years" with "100 Red Tourism Routes of CPC 100th Anniversary", 6 red scenic spots are among the key ones for Sichuan's development of red tourism; 13 units are among the first revolutionary education research and practice bases in Sichuan's primary and secondary schools, and 6 units are the social practice education bases for Sichuan's youth; 3 airlines are among the first major airlines for national red scenic spots, and the first national red-themed expressway has been opened to traffic - Zhenba-Guang'an Expressway (Wangping-Tongjiang Section); 6 national AAAA-level tourist attractions are supported by red tourism resources, 5 red tourism routes such as "Sichuan-Shaanxi Soviet Area, Travel Restarted from the Heart", and 13 research, study and travel routes have been put forward, 41 characteristic research and study travel bases and camps built, and the series of routes of "Walk the Road, Eat the Food, Wear the Uniforms, Watch the Dramas, Sing the Songs, and Visit the Cities as Red Army Has ever Done" have been developed in addition to the like cultural tourism brands.

红四方面军总指挥部旧址纪念馆
1932–2022
纪念川陕革命根据地
创建90周年
争创天府旅游名县
推动全域旅游

红四方面军总指挥部旧址纪念馆

红四方面军总指挥部旧址纪念馆位于通江县诺江镇文庙街，是全国重点文物保护单位、全国爱国主义教育示范基地、全国 100 个红色旅游经典景区和 30 条红色精品旅游线路之一，国家 AAA 级旅游景区，是“不忘初心、牢记使命”主题教育、爱国主义教育和革命传统教育的重要阵地。景区有红四方面军总指挥部旧址、总政治部旧址，列宁公园，中共川陕省委党校旧址，川陕省委遗址等，展出收藏各类文物 7800 余件，可游览面积 3 万余平方米。其中，列宁公园是用外国领袖名字命名的革命纪念公园。纪念馆馆舍原为通江文庙和学宫，始建于宋嘉祐七年（1062），建筑依山就势，呈梯形布局，造型凝重，结构严谨，艺术性和观赏性很高，是川东北保存较为完整的古建筑之一。

Memorial Hall of Former Site of Fourth Front Red Army's General Headquarters

This memorial hall, located in Confucian Temple Street, Nuojiang Town, Tongjiang County as a major historical and cultural site protected at the national level, a national model base for patriotism education, one of the top 100 key spots for red tourism and 30 key routes for red tourism and a AAA-level tourist attraction, is a key venue for the themed education of "Stay true to our original aspiration and founding mission", of patriotism and of revolutionary tradition. It has scenic spots such as former sites of both General Headquarters and General Political Department of the Fourth Front Red Army, Lenin Park, of CPC Sichuan-Shaanxi Provincial Committee Party School, and of Sichuan-Shaanxi Provincial Party Committee. Over 7,800 cultural relics of various types are exhibited and its touring area covers over 30,000 square meters. Among them, Lenin Park is a revolutionary memorial park in memory of the Soviet Union leader Lenin. This memorial hall, built along the mountain in the seventh year of Jiayou in the Song Dynasty (1062), had once been Tongjiang Confucian Temple and School. With a trapezoidal layout, dignified shape and rigorous structure, it has a great artistic and ornamental sense, hence a well-preserved ancient building in Northeastern Sichuan.

许洪伟 / 摄
红四方面军总指挥部旧址纪念馆

Photo / Xu Hongwei
Memorial Hall of Former Site of Fourth Front Red Army's General Headquarters

张学金 / 摄
通江列宁公园

Photo / Zhang Xuejin
Tongjiang Lenin Park

张学金 / 摄
中共川陕省委党校旧址

Photo / Zhang Xuejin
Former Site of Party School of CPC Sichuan-Shaanxi Provincial Committee

川陕革命根据地红军烈士陵园管理局供图 Photo / Courtesy of Red Army Martyrs Cemetery Administration for Sichuan-Shaanxi Revolutionary Base Area

红四方面军总医院旧址

Former Site of Fourth Front Red Army's General Hospital

张学金 / 摄 Photo / Zhang Xuejin

位于川陕革命根据地红军烈士陵园的纪念馆

Memorial Hall of Red Army Martyrs Cemetery in Sichuan-Shaanxi Revolutionary Base

川陕革命根据地博物馆

川陕革命根据地博物馆位于巴中市巴州区南龛山旅游景区（国家 AAAA 级旅游景区），是全国爱国主义教育示范基地、全国青少年教育基地、国防教育示范基地、全国红色旅游经典景区、四川省爱国主义教育基地、四川省干部教育培训现场教学点、全国首批免费开放的博物馆、国家三级博物馆、四川博物院流动博物馆巴中分馆。博物馆占地面积 16032.78 平方米，建筑面积 4707 平方米，是收藏、研究、展示、宣传中国工农红军第四方面军和川陕苏区历史的综合性博物馆，有馆藏文物资料 2 万余件，其中国家一级文物 11 件。

Museum of Sichuan-Shaanxi Revolutionary Base

This museum, located in Bazhong's Mt. South Niche, Bazhou District, is a national AAAA-level scenic area for red tourism, and education base for national patriotism, youth, and national defense, National Red Tourism Classic Scenic Spot, Sichuan Provincial Patriotism Education Base, Sichuan Provincial Cadre Education and Training On-Site Teaching Point, China's first free and open museums, a national third-class museum, and Bazhong Branch of Sichuan Mobile Museum. With an area of about 16 thousand square meters (4,707 square meters of built-in area), this comprehensive museum, meant for collecting, researching, displaying and promoting the history of the Fourth Front Red Army and of the Sichuan-Shaanxi Soviet Area, owns over 20,000 cultural relics and related materials, 11 of which are among the national first-class ones.

张学金 / 摄
川陕革命根据地博物馆

Photo / Zhang Xuejin
Museum of Sichuan-Shaanxi Revolutionary Base

智勇坚定 排难创新
团结奋斗 不胜不休

川陕苏区将帅碑林

川陕苏区将帅碑林位于巴中市巴州区南龛山旅游景区（国家 AAAA 级旅游景区），是全国爱国主义教育示范基地、全国生态文明教育示范基地、四川省爱国主义教育基地、四川省国防教育基地、四川统一战线中国特色社会主义教育基地、中国最大的红军碑林。建有红四方面军主要将领纪念像园、红军将士个人纪念单碑长廊、红军将士英名纪念碑（巴中市烈士公祭广场）、将帅碑林纪念馆、红色组雕等 20 余处景观。安放“歼六”战斗机 1 架，“三七”高炮 2 门。栽植名贵树木 1 万余株。长廊内嵌碑 6000 余块，英名纪念碑刻红军烈士名录 13.8 万人。征集中央首长、高级将领题词 500 余件，收集红军将士捐献纪念物品 10535 件。

Stele Forest for Soldiers and Officers with Sichuan-Shaanxi Soviet Area

This stele forest, located in Mt. South Niche Tourist area, Bazhou District, Bazhong, is the largest of its kind for the Red Army in China, and also a national AAAA-level tourist scenic area, a national demonstration base for patriotism education, a national demonstration base for ecological protection education, and a provincial base for patriotism education, a national defense education base, and a united front socialist education base with Chinese Characteristics. There exist 20-plus landscapes such as the Memorial Statue Garden of the Chief Generals of the Fourth Front Red Army, the Corridor of Single Memorial Monuments to the Red Armymen, the Monument to the Red Army Soldiers and Officers (Bazhong City Martyrs Memorial Square), the Memorial Hall of Generals in the Stele Forest, and the red sculptures. One J-6 fighter jet and two 37mm anti-aircraft artillery pieces are placed. More than 10,000 precious trees are planted. Over 6,000 steles are embedded in the Corridor, and 138,000 illustrious names of Red Army martyrs engraved on the monument. Above 500 inscriptions from leaders of the central authorities and senior generals have been collected in addition to around 10,535 commemorative items donated by the Red Army soldiers and officers.

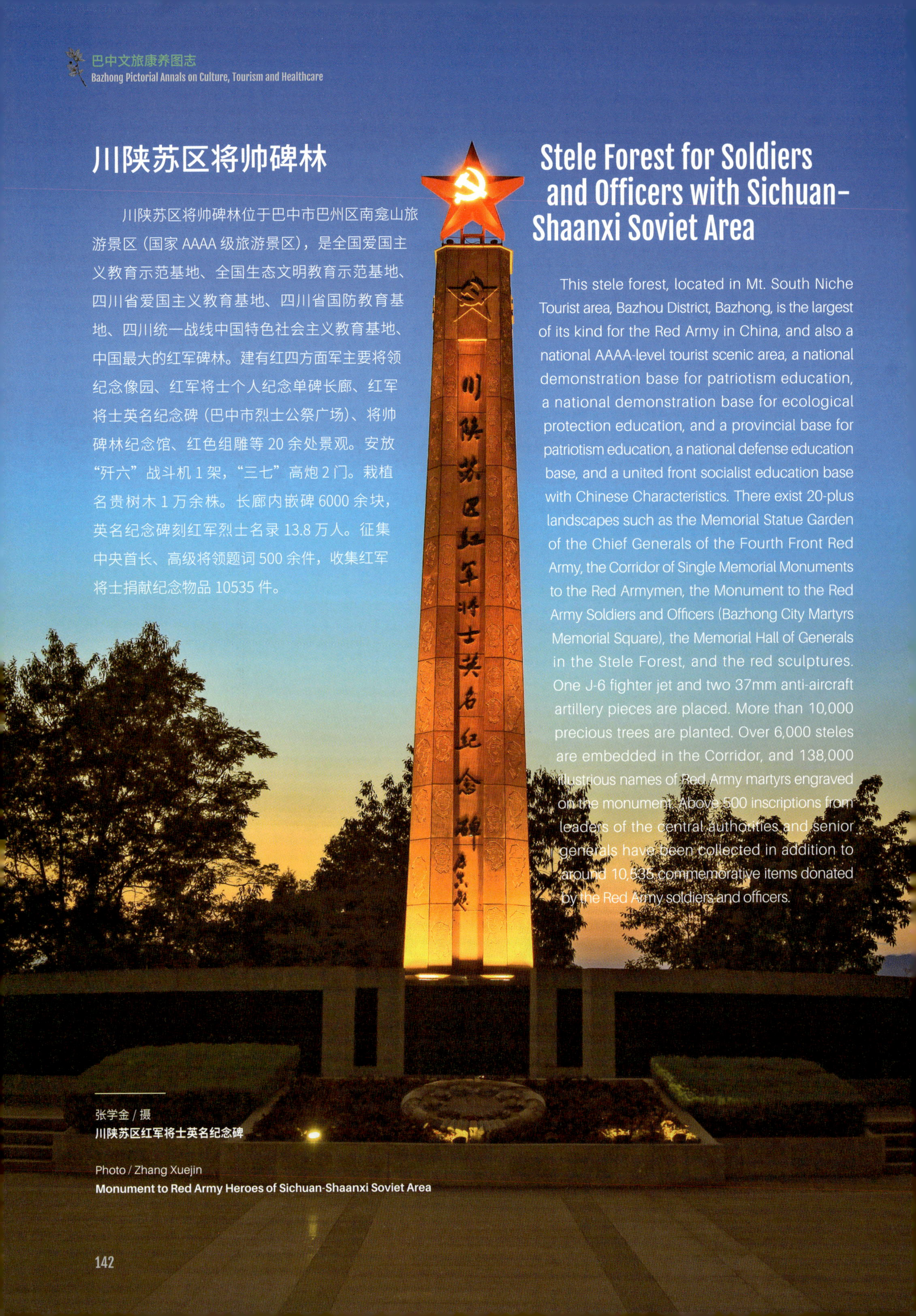

张学金 / 摄
川陕苏区红军将士英名纪念碑

Photo / Zhang Xuejin
Monument to Red Army Heroes of Sichuan-Shaanxi Soviet Area

张学金 / 摄
红四方面军主要将领纪念像园

Photo / Zhang Xuejin
Commemorative Statue Park for Chief Generals of the Fourth Front Red Army

川陕革命根据地博物馆供图
红军将士个人纪念单碑长廊

Photo / Courtesy of Sichuan-Shaanxi Revolutionary Base Museum
Corridor of Single Memorial Monuments to Red Army Soldiers and Officers

上图　平昌县文广旅局供图
中国工农红军石刻标语园红军标语长廊
下图　平昌县文广旅局供图
中国工农红军石刻标语园

Above Photo / Courtesy of Pingchang Bureau of Culture, Radio and Tourism
Corridor for Stone-Carved Slogan Garden of Chinese Workers' and Peasants' Red Army
Below Photo / Courtesy of Pingchang Bureau of Culture, Radio and Tourism
Stone-Carved Slogan Garden of Chinese Workers' and Peasants' Red Army

中国工农红军石刻标语园

中国工农红军石刻标语园位于平昌县佛头山国家 AAAA 级旅游景区内，占地 200 余亩，是以红军石刻标语为主题的红色旅游景区，共收录展示了土地革命战争时期全国 10 余个苏区 16 个省、79 个县、1600 余幅红军石刻标语。标语园有红旗广场、红军标语长廊、绿化景观区、红军街等片区，石刻类、墨书类、漫画类三大主题展示区域，设政治发动、经济社会、军事斗争、文化教育四大主题，集历史性、文化性、教育性、休闲性于一体，是群众强身健体的主题公园，又是红色文化观光旅游景区和爱国主义教育基地。

Stone-Carved Slogan Garden of Chinese Workers' and Peasants' Red Army

This garden, located in the National AAAA-level tourist scenic area of Mt. Fotou, Pingchang County, which covers an area of over 13 hectares, has displayed over 1,600 stone-carved slogans (by the red army during the Agrarian Revolutionary War) collected from a dozen Soviet areas scattered in 16 provinces and 79 counties. Composed of Red Flag Square, Red Army Slogan Corridor, Green Landscape Area, and Red Army Street, it shows such three themed displays as stone carvings, ink works and comics concerning four aspects such as political publicity, economic society, military struggle, and cultural education, which integrates history, culture, education and leisure, hence a theme park for the masses, a red tourism scenic spot and a patriotism education base.

刘伯坚纪念馆

刘伯坚纪念馆位于平昌县佛头山国家 AAAA 级旅游景区，被列入全国红色旅游经典景区名录，是全国 100 个红色旅游经典景区和 30 条红色精品旅游线路之一、四川省爱国主义教育基地、四川省文物保护单位。纪念馆占地面积 22387 平方米，由刘伯坚烈士纪念碑诗屏、碑廊和刘伯坚烈士生平事迹陈列馆组成，陈列刘伯坚烈士遗物 1000 余件。

Liu Bojian Memorial Hall

This hall, located in the national AAAA-level tourist scenic area of Pingchang's Mt. Fotou, is included in the List of National Classic Red Tourism Scenic Spots, one of China's 100 classic red tourism scenic spots and, 30 red tourist routes, Sichuan patriotism education base and Sichuan Provincial Cultural Relics for Preservation. With an area of 22,387 square meters, it consists of a poem screen, a monument gallery, and an exhibition hall of the martyr's life story with 1,000-plus pieces of his belongings.

平昌县委党史研究室供图 Photo / Courtesy of Party History Research Office, Pingchang

刘伯坚纪念馆 **Liubojian Memorial Hall**

巴山游击队纪念馆

巴山游击队纪念馆位于巴中市文旅新区光雾山镇铁炉坝村，占地3700平方米，是全国100个红色旅游经典景区和30条红色精品旅游线路之一、四川省党性教育基地、四川省爱国主义教育基地、巴中市廉洁文化基地。纪念馆包括巴山游击队指挥部旧址、巴山游击队史迹陈列室、巴山游击队队长赵明恩烈士墓、南江革命史陈列室、南江古文化长廊、“铁骨忠魂”主题雕塑及广场等，展陈文物157件（套），其中国家珍贵文物22件（套）。

Memorial Hall of Bashan Guerrilla

This memorial hall of 3,700 square meters, located in Tieluba Village, Bazhong's Guangwushan Town, Cultural Tourism New Area as one of China's 100 classic red tourism scenic spots and, 30 red tourist routes, is a cultural base for the education of the Party, patriotism and Bazhong's clean government as well. It includes the former site of Bashan Guerrilla Headquarters, Bashan Exhibition Room for Guerrilla Historical Relics, Tomb of Guerrilla Leader and Martyr Zhao Ming'en, Nanjiang Revolutionary History Exhibition Room, Nanjiang Ancient Culture Corridor, "Iron Bones and Loyal Soul" themed sculptures and squares, and exhibits 157 pieces (sets) of cultural relics, 22 of them being national precious ones.

张学金 / 摄
巴山游击队纪念馆

Photo / Zhang Xuejin
Memorial Hall of Bashan Guerrilla

中国历史文化名镇——毛浴镇

毛浴镇位于通江县城东北部，是中国历史文化名镇、四川最美古镇，也是红四方面军训词诞生地。明清两代，毛浴镇皆为川东北军事重镇。1934 年，红四方面军在毛浴镇召开全军党政工作会议，诞生了“智勇坚定、排难创新、团结奋斗、不胜不休”十六字训词。镇上保存有完好的红四方面军党政工作会议遗址，中共赤江县委、县苏维埃政府遗址，红军石刻标语墙，列宁小学，红军树及红军拴马林等红色遗址，其中红军石刻标语墙为全国重点文物保护单位。毛浴镇迎春村为中国传统村落。

Maoyu, a Chinese Historical and Cultural Town

Maoyu, located in the northeast of Tongjiang County, is a historical and cultural town in China and one of Sichuan's most beautiful ancient towns. During the Ming and Qing dynasties, it was an important military place in northeastern Sichuan. In 1934, a 16-character precept meaning "Courageous and Determined, Undaunted and Innovative, United and Hardworking, Ongoing till Victorious" was born of the Fourth Front Red Army at its Party and government work conference held in this town, the site of which is still well-preserved, in addition to those of CPC Chijiang County Party Committee and Soviet Government, Lenin Primary School, Red Army trees and forest for tying horses, and Red Army's Stone-Carved Slogan Wall, the last of which being a national Key cultural relic for preservation. Maoyu's Yingchun is a traditional Chinese village.

上图　张平供图
毛浴古镇全景
下图　张学金 / 摄
毛浴古镇红军石刻标语墙

Above Photo / Zhang Ping
Whole View of Maoyu Ancient Town
Below Photo / Zhang Xuejin
Red Army's Stone Slogan in Maoyu Ancient Town

擁護中國共產主義青年團
實行共產主義打倒國民政府

第三章

城市旅游

巴中市辖 3 个县、2 个区、2 个经开区和 1 个文旅融合发展示范区，是秦巴山片区中心城市、全国革命老区重点城市，是中国气候养生之都、国家卫生城市、国家森林城市、全国双拥模范城、全国生态文明城市、国家生态文明建设示范区、全国旅游标准化示范单位、全国最美生态宜居典范城市、四川省园林城市、全省旅游标准化示范市。

巴中历史悠久，文化底蕴深厚，旅游资源富集，巴人文化、秦汉文化、三国文化、隋唐文化、红色文化、民俗文化交相辉映，拥有“巴文化中心、川陕苏区首府、晏阳初故里”三张文化名片，“山水、洞天、红色、人文、康养”五张金字招牌，“川陕苏区首府，秦巴生态名城”城市名片和“诗意山水，红色巴中”旅游名片。

市中心城区和 3 个市域副中心城市旅游异彩纷呈，千年米仓古道纵贯全境，巴中石窟被誉为“国之瑰宝”，恩阳古镇建筑极具川东北民居风格，正月十六登高、皮影戏等优秀传统文化薪火相传，通江银耳节、“恩阳船说”夜游演出等仪式活动独具特色，彰显了中国历史文化名镇、四川省历史文化名城、天府旅游名县的独特魅力。厚重优美的城市旅游景点、特色休闲街区、文创景观小品、夜间消费中心展现了多业态城市旅游功能，铺展了“城在山中建、水在城中走、楼在绿中立、人在景中游”的城市旅游山水画卷。

全新的巴中城市 logo、市树市花等城市形象标识，“智勇坚定、排难创新、团结奋斗、不胜不休”的新时代巴中城市精神，让巴中城市旅游品位和知名度不断提升。“宜居、宜业、宜商、宜游，有颜值、有品位、有温度、有活力”现代化新城的城市旅游日渐凸显。

张学金 / 摄
南龛山景区

Photo / Zhang Xuejin
Mt. South Niche

Chapter 3

Urban Tourism

Bazhong, with 3 counties, 2 districts, 2 economic development zones and 1 demonstration zone for the integrated development of culture and tourism under its jurisdiction, is the central city of the Qinling-Bashan Mountains, and a key city in China's old revolutionary bases in addition to the capital of healthcare, city of national sanitation, national forest, ecological civilization, National Ecological Civilization Construction Demonstration Zone, tourism standardization demonstration, most beautiful ecological and livable model, Sichuan garden city, and so on.

Bazhong has a long history of profound cultural heritage, rich tourism resources, Ba people culture, Qin and Han culture, Three Kingdoms culture, Sui and Tang culture, Revolutionary Culture, and folk culture ,and possesses such 3 cultural brandnames as Center of Ba Culture, Capital of Sichuan-Shaanxi-Soviet Area and Hometown of Yan Yangchu", 5 other tourism brands of "landscape, cave, red tourism, culture and healthcare" besides its great fame of "Capital of Sichuan-Shaanxi-Soviet Area and Well-Known Qinling-Bashan Ecological City" and "Poetic Landscape and Heroic Bazhong".

Its downtown area and 3 sub-center cities are splendid in tourism; Micang Ancient Road runs all through the area; Bazhong Grottoes are known as a "national treasure"; Enyang Ancient Town typical of Sichuan's Northeastern dwelling style, hill-climbing on the 16th of the first month in Chinese Lunar New Year and excellent traditional cultures such as shadow play have been passed down from generation to generation; activities such as Tongjiang Tremella Festival and "Enyang Boat Talk" night tour are unique, which highlights the unusual charms of China's famous historical and cultural towns, Sichuan's famous historical, and tourist cultural cities/counties. The rich and beautiful urban tourist attractions, characteristic leisure blocks, creative and cultural landscape sketches, and night consumption centers show the multi-format urban tourism function and a landscape of a scroll of "city standing in the mountain, water flowing through the city, buildings in the greenery and, people moving in the scenery".

Bazhong's brand-new city logo, city tree and city flower and so on, and its new-era city spirit of "Courageous and Determined; Undaunted and Innovative; United and Hardworking; Ongoing till Victorious" have been greatly improving its tourism taste and popularity. The urban tourism of a modern new city, which is "suitable for living, work, business, and tourism, as well as good-looking, tasteful, warm, and energetic" has become increasingly prominent.

上图　张学金 / 摄
人民广场
下图　张学金 / 摄
南池艺术广场

Above Photo / Zhang Xuejin
People's Square
Below Photo / Zhang Xuejin
Nanchi Art Plaza

张学金 / 摄
巴人广场

Photo / Zhang Xuejin
Ba People's Square

晏阳初博物馆

晏阳初博物馆位于巴中城郊塔子山顶，是中国华侨国际文化交流基地、巴中市爱国主义教育基地、巴中市社会科学普及基地、巴中市廉政文化教育基地。博物馆总占地约 42666.67 平方米，由晏阳初博士史迹展览馆、晏阳初墓、晏阳初博士汉白玉塑像、巴中名人园、董修武墓及凌云塔等景观构成。馆藏文物及文献资料 2461 件（册），是全国宣传晏阳初平民教育思想和乡村改造运动理论中规模最大、馆藏文物最丰富的博物馆，为宣传展示晏阳初平民教育思想、研究平民教育理论的重要基地。

Museum of YanYangchu

This museum, located on the top of Tazi Peak in the suburbs of Bazhong, is China International Cultural Exchange Base for Overseas Chinese, a patriotism education base, a social science popularization base, and a clean government education base. With a total area of about 42,666.67 square meters, it consists of Dr. Yan Yangchu's historical relics exhibition hall, tomb, white marble statue, Bazhong Celebrity Garden, Dong Xiuwu's tomb and Lingyun Pagoda. Its 2,461 volumes of cultural relics and documents make the largest and richest collection of cultural relics for the nationwide publicity of Yan Yangchu's philosophy and theory of civilian education.

张学金 / 摄
晏阳初博物馆

Photo / Zhang Xuejin
Museum of Yan Yangchu

南龛山旅游景区

南龛山旅游景区位于巴中市巴州区南龛山，是国家 AAAA 级旅游景区。景区有南龛摩崖造像、南龛公园、川陕革命根据地博物馆及川陕苏区将帅碑林等景点，集红色文化、佛教文化、民俗文化、历史文化、生态文化于一体。其中，南龛摩崖造像为全国重点文物保护单位。景区有题壁诗文数百条，李白曾书“怪状”二字镌刻于此。南龛公园风景秀丽，水杉、雪松、黑壳楠、银杏、露经柏、苏铁等 150 余种乔灌木林及名贵花卉生长于此，飞霞阁、梓桐宫、南池、望州亭等景观令人流连忘返。

李维建 / 摄
飞霞阁景点

Photo / Li Weijian
Feixia Pavilion

Mt. South Niche

This national AAAA-level tourist scenic area, located in Bazhong's Bazhou District, includes South Niche Cliff Statues, South Niche Park, Museum of Sichuan-Shaanxi Revolutionary Base, Stele Forest for Soldiers and Officers with Sichuan-Shaanxi Soviet Area. It integrates Revolutionary Culture, Buddhist culture, folk culture, historical culture and ecological culture. Among them, the colorful carvings of the prime-time Tang Dynasty on the South Niche cliffs are national key cultural relics for preservation. It has hundreds of poems scribed on the wall, and the words of "strange shape" by Li Bai still remains here. Beautiful is South Niche Park, with 150 and more species of trees, shrubs and precious flowers such as metasequoia, cedar, lindera megaphylla, ginkgo, cypress and cycad, where Feixia Pavilion, Zitong Palace, Nanchi Pool, and Wangzhou Pavilion are most unforgettable.

凌云塔

凌云塔位于巴中市城郊塔子山顶，建于清道光十年（1830）。八边形塔身，砖石结构，十三层楼阁式，八角攒尖顶。该塔高 43.33 米，由地宫、基座、塔身、塔刹四部分组成，气势雄伟，造型美观，保存完好。

回风亭

回风亭位于巴中市巴州区回风街道办事处，始建于 1926 年，1928 年竣工落成。回风亭建筑面积 210 平方米，坐南朝北，平面呈正八边形，共五层，通高 31 米。该亭采用中西建筑结合方式构建，是巴中较具特色的标志性建筑之一。

Lingyun Pagoda

Located on the top of Tazi Peak in the suburbs of Bazhong, it was built in the 10th year (1830) of Daoguang, Qing Dynasty. Octagonal from body till spire, and of masonry structure, which is majestic and beautifully-shaped and well preserved, this thirteen-story pagoda consists of four parts (underground palace, base, body and brake), a total height of 43.33 meters.

Huifeng Pavilion

This pavilion, located in Bazhong's Huifeng Subdistrict, Bazhou District, was started in 1926, and completed two years later. It occupies an area of 210 square meters. Facing south, it is a regular octagon of five floors in all and of 31 meters in height. As a building of Chinese and Western architecture, it is one of the unique landmark buildings in Bazhong.

1　王志刚 / 摄
回风亭夜景
2　张学金 / 摄
凌云塔
3　李振豪 / 供图
巴中市巴州区历史文化博物馆

1. Photo / Wang Zhigang
Night View from Huifeng Pavilion
2. Photo / Zhang Xuejin
Lingyun Pagoda
3. Photo / Li Zhenhao
Bazhou Museum of History and Culture, Bazhong

1

2

3

张学金 / 摄
恩阳古镇鸟瞰

Photo / Zhang Xuejin
Aerial View of Enyang Ancient Town

中国历史文化名镇——恩阳古镇

恩阳古镇位于巴中市恩阳区，是国家 AAAA 级旅游景区、中国历史文化名镇、国家级生态乡镇、全国文明村镇、2021 中国最具品质文化旅游胜地、2022 美丽中国首选目的地、四川十大古镇、四川最美古镇、天府旅游名镇、四川文创集市、四川省文旅特色小镇、巴蜀文化旅游走廊新地标。

古镇历史悠久，自南北朝梁武帝置义阳郡开始建制，旧时衔接米仓古道，对接陕渝物流的水码头和物资集散中心，是米仓古道上繁华的集镇，素有“小武汉”“小上海”美称。恩阳是纳入米仓古道申遗的唯一古镇，也是世界双遗产“蜀道”的重要构成部分。

古镇核心面积 50 万平方米，有 18 条古街巷、589 幢成片保存完好的明清时期古建筑群，堪称川东北民居艺术精品；有厚重的巴人文化、恩义文化、米仓古道文化、佛教文化、红军文化、名人文化等文化资源，历史底蕴深厚；有万寿宫、起凤桥、水码头、米仓古道南段遗址等古遗址，胡家大院、大栈房、红军经理处等红军文化遗址，均为全国重点文物保护单位；有巴中文化创意产业园、问心堂、花间堂精品民宿等文旅项目，打造了“恩阳船说”大型夜游演出项目；有恩阳十大碗、提糖麻饼等特色美食。

右图　张学金 / 摄　Right Photo / Zhang Xuejin
恩阳古镇起凤桥　**Qifeng Bridge in Enyang Ancient Town**
左一图　张学金 / 摄　Photo (First from Left) / Zhang Xuejin
恩阳古镇万寿宫　**Longevity Palace, Enyang Ancient Town**
左二图　张学金 / 摄　Photo (Second from Left) / Zhang Xuejin
恩阳古镇大栈房　**Big Roadhouse, Enyang Ancient Town**

Enyang Ancient Town, a Historical and Cultural One in China

Located in Bazhong's Enyang District, it is a national AAAA-level tourist scenic area, historical, cultural, ecological, and advanced town, China's 2021 most high-quality cultural tourism destination, 2022 beautiful preferred destination, Sichuan's top ten ancient town, creative and cultural market, cultural and tourism characteristic town, and new landmark of Bashu Cultural Tourism Corridor.

This scenic spot, since the establishment of Yiyang County by Emperor Liangwu of the Southern and Northern Dynasties, was in former times connected to Micang Ancient Road as the port center of goods for Shaanxi and Chongqing, hence the name of "Smaller Wuhan/Shanghai". It was once the only ancient town connected to Micang Ancient Road, and so an important part of the world double heritage concerning " Ancient Shu Road".

Its core area is 500,000 square meters with 18 ancient streets and 589 well-preserved ancient buildings in the Ming and Qing Dynasties, which can be called the fine arts of the northeastern Sichuan dwellings; Ba people's culture, Enyi (gratitude) culture, Micang ancient road culture, Buddhist culture, Red Army culture, and celebrity culture make a profound historical heritage; ancient sites such as Longevity Palace, Qifeng Bridge, Wharf, ruins of the southern section of Micang Ancient Road, Hu Family Courtyard, Big Roadhouse, Red Army cultural relics are all under national key preservation; there are cultural and tourism projects such as Bazhong Creative and Cultural Industry Park, Wenxintang, and Huajiantang key Homestay, besides some large-scale night tour performances like *The Legend of Enyang*, and special dishes such as Enyang Ten Dishes and Sugared Sesame Cakes.

左图　巴中日报社供图
恩阳登科公园
右图　张学金 / 摄
恩阳大梁山城市公园未来之眼景点

Left Photo / Courtesy of Bazhong Daily
Dengke Park, Enyang
Right Photo / Zhang Xuejin
Eye of the Future in Daliangshan City Park, Enyang

小图　九寨山风景区管委会供图
九寨山景区巴山秋池景点
大图　四川秦巴新城投资集团供图
九寨山景区

Small Photo / Courtesy of Mt Jiuzhai Scenic Area Management Committee
Qiuchi Scenic Spot, Bashan, Mt. Jiuzhai Scenic Area
Big Photo / Courtesy of Qinba New City Investment Group, Sichuan
Mt. Jiuzhai Scenic Area

九寨山旅游景区

九寨山旅游景区位于巴中经开区，是国家 AAAA 级旅游景区。景区面积 1168 万平方米，森林覆盖率超过 70%，有巴山秋池、莲花寨、农耕博物馆、文化长廊、上山栈道等景点。景区是中国西部首个城市新区、产业园区和旅游景区三区同建实验性项目，融全域旅游、城市建设、文化传承于一体。

Mt. Jiuzhai Scenic Area

This national AAAA-level tourist scenic area is located in Bazhong Economic and Technological Development Zone, with a coverage of 11.68 million square meters, and a forest coverage rate of over 70%. It has such spots as Bashan Autumn Pond, Lotus Village, Agricultural Museum, Cultural Corridor and Uphill Plank Road, and is the first experimental project of co-construction of three districts, including a new urban area, an industrial park and a tourist attraction in West China, integrating global tourism, urban construction and cultural heritage.

1	3
2	

1　吴文圣 / 摄
南江廊桥
2　杜远平 / 摄
南江宏帆广场
3　巴中日报社供图
南江养生潭湿地公园

1. Photo / Wu Wensheng
Covered Bridge, Nanjiang
2. Photo / Du Yuanping
Hongfan Plaza, Nanjiang
3. Photo / Courtesy of Bazhong Daily
Healthcare Wetland Park, Nanjiang

1

2

3

中国通江银耳博物馆

中国通江银耳博物馆位于通江县高明新区核心区域，具有宣传通江银耳文化、保护通江银耳文物等功能，集生产、学习、研究、市场、旅游等于一体，为“四川省科普教育基地”。博物馆占地 40050 平方米，建筑面积 6000 平方米，由“主馆”“天地之灵”“雾露之间”“青杠林里”“银耳人家”“形象广场”六个部分组成。其中，展厅面积 3700 余平方米，由“神奇自然 天赐”“培育奇珍 地孕”“耳香悠远 人文”“商贸之道 和合”“灵滋妙补 神效”“乐美蓝图 乐享”“珍馐美韵 品鉴”七大展区及 3D 数字影院组成。

Tongjiang Tremella Museum of China

This museum, located in the core area of Tongjiang's Gaoming New Area as a base for science popularization education in Sichuan, is meant for publicizing and preserving the local tremella culture and cultural relics by integrating production, learning, research, market, and tourism. Of its 40,050 square meters, 6,000 of which is built-in area, it is composed of six parts: Main Hall, Essence from Nature, Mist and Dew, Quercus Semicarpifolia Forest, Tremella Cultivator and Image Square. Its exhibition hall of over 3,700 square meters is made up of such 7 pavilions as Magical Nature, Priceless Treasure, Renowned Fragrance, Commercial Trade, Magical Effect, Great Enjoyment and Tasty Feel in addition to a 3D digital cinema.

1 巴中日报社供图
通江红军广场
2 巴中日报社供图
通江高明湖湿地公园
3 巴中日报社供图
通江壁山森林公园
4 中国通江银耳博物馆供图
中国通江银耳博物馆

1. Photo / Courtesy of Bazhong Daily
Red Army Square, Tongjiang
2. Photo / Courtesy of Bazhong Daily
Gaoming Lake Wetland Park, Tongjiang
3. Photo / Courtesy of Bazhong Daily
Bishan Forest Park, Tongjiang
4. Photo / Courtesy of China Tongjiang Tremella Museum
Tongjiang Tremella Museum of China

4

佛头山旅游景区

佛头山旅游景区位于平昌县城北侧，是国家 AAAA 级旅游景区。景区总面积 2360 万平方米，以红色文化、佛教文化、民俗文化三大文化区为核心。红色文化区主要有刘伯坚纪念馆、刘伯坚烈士纪念碑、中国工农红军石刻标语园、红色文化长廊等；佛教文化区主要有佛山寺、华严寺、极乐寺等；民俗文化区主要有巴人民俗文化园、米仓古道遗迹等。该景区是集休闲度假、民俗体验、佛教朝觐、红色教育、旅游观光于一体的旅游景区、文化园区。

Mt. Fotou

This national AAAA-level tourist scenic area, which totals 23.6 million square meters, is located in the north of Pingchang and centers on the three major aspects of Red Culture, Buddhist culture and folk culture: the first includes Memorial Hall of Monument to Liu Bojian, Liubojian Monument to Martyrs, Red Army's Stone-Carved Slogan Garden and Red Cultural Corridor; the second includes such temples as Foshan, Huayan and Jile; and the third includes Ba Folk Cultural Garden, and remains of Micang Ancient Road. It is a tourist scenic area and cultural park integrating leisure and vacation, folk experience, Buddhist pilgrimage, red education, and tourism.

王建华 / 摄
平昌佛头山景区

Photo / Wang Jianhua
Mt. Fotou, Pingchang

第四章

乡村旅游

顾志平 / 摄
山水化湖景区暮色

Photo / Gu Zhiping
Twilight at Shanshuihuahu

巴中乡村旅游资源丰富，地方特色浓郁，乡村旅游产品业态多样，巴中市恩阳区、平昌县为全国“绿水青山就是金山银山”实践创新基地，有全国休闲农业与乡村旅游示范县 1 个、中国美丽休闲乡村 4 个、全国文明村镇 15 个、中国乡村旅游模范村 2 个、中国乡村旅游模范户 2 户、中国乡村旅游金牌农家乐 5 家、中国乡村旅游致富带头人 23 人；有四川省乡村旅游示范县 2 个、四川省乡村旅游强县 1 个、四川省乡村旅游重点村 8 个、四川省乡村旅游示范乡镇 19 个、四川省乡村旅游示范村 67 个、星级农家乐或乡村酒店 117 家；还有南江县、通江县等天府旅游名县及天府旅游名镇、名村、名宿等多个。有以乡村旅游为核心的国家 AAAA 级旅游景区 3 个、中国传统村落 27 个、四川省传统村落 99 个。

巴中举办乡村旅游文化节、茶文化旅游节等特色文化节庆活动，凭借农业园区、森林景观、乡村聚落、水利风景、古镇新村等多种乡村旅游资源，打造了以水文化、孝道文化、红色文化、佛教文化、道教文化、鱼文化、林文化等为主题的乡村旅游品牌，发展休闲观光、采摘体验、农事体验、农家休闲、民俗展示、亲子旅游等乡村旅游新业态，成为集农业、观光、休闲于一体的乡村旅游目的地。

Chapter 4

Rural Tourism

Bazhong is rich in rural tourism resources, typical of local characteristics, and various in rural tourism products, its Enyang District and Pingchang County are bases for the national innovative practice of "Clean Waters and Green Mountains as Invaluable Assets". It owns 1 national leisure agriculture and rural tourism demonstration county, 4 Chinese beautiful leisure villages, 15 national advanced villages and towns, and 2 Chinese rural tourism model villages; 2 model households of rural tourism, 5 gold medal farmhouses in rural tourism, and 23 leaders of rural tourism across the country; 2 rural tourism demonstration counties, 1 strong rural tourism county, and 8 key rural tourism villages, and 19 respectively rural tourism demonstration towns and villages in Sichuan, 67 rural

tourism demonstration villages throughout Sichuan, and 117 star-rated farmhouses or country hotels; Sichuan's famous tourist towns, Sichuan's famous tourist villages, and Sichuan's famous tourist hotels, 3 national AAAA-level tourist scenic areas with rural tourism as the core, 27 traditional Chinese villages and 99 traditional villages in Sichuan.

Bazhong holds special cultural festivals such as rural tourism culture and tea culture tourism. Based on rural tourism resources such as agricultural parks, forest landscapes, rural settlements, water conservancy landscapes, ancient towns and new villages, it has created water culture, filial piety culture, rural tourism brands with the theme of revolutionary culture, Buddhist culture, Taoist culture, fishing culture and forest culture, have developed such new forms of rural tourism as leisure sightseeing, experiences as fruit-picking and farming, farm leisure, folk custom display, and parent-child tourism, and become a destination with agriculture, sightseeing and leisure integrated.

山水化湖旅游景区

山水化湖旅游景区位于巴中市巴州区化成镇，是国家 AAAA 级旅游景区、国家水利风景区。景区水域面积 312 万平方米，为文化、旅游、生产、生活、服务功能有机结合的特色文化生态观光休闲景区。景区所在地化成镇（连厢）为四川省民间文化艺术之乡，化城镇长潭河村为四川省第二批省级乡村旅游重点村，白庙村为国家森林乡村。

张学金 / 摄
山水化湖旅游景区鸟瞰

Photo / Zhang Xuejin
Aerial View of Shanshuihua Lake

Shanshuihua Lake

Located in Bazhong's Huacheng Town, Bazhou District, it is a national AAAA-level tourist and water conservancy scenic area with a water coverage of 3.12 million square meters, which is intended for cultural, ecological, sightseeing and leisure with the organic integration of culture, tourism, production, life and services. Huacheng, where the scenic spot is located, is home to Sichuan folk culture and art, and its, Changtanhe is among the second key provincial-level rural tourism villages, and Baimiao a national forest village.

万寿养生谷旅游景区

万寿养生谷旅游景区位于巴中市恩阳区下八庙镇万寿村，是国家 AAAA 级旅游景区、四川省森林康养基地、四川省首批乡村旅游重点村。景区面积 2800 万平方米，主要有万寿湖水利风景区、玫瑰文化产业园、国家农业科技园三大景点。景区内群山秀丽，湖水幽美，古宅俨然，有“巴山民宿”群落、村史馆、寿文化展览馆、龟鹤齐寿、怡寿廊等景观，具有深厚的长寿文化、祈福文化、民俗文化、农耕文化、食药同源文化底蕴，是养生健体、休闲度假、生态观光、科普教育基地。万寿村的张家院子民宿为天府旅游名宿，万寿村为国家森林乡村、中国美丽休闲乡村。

左图　付海旭 / 摄
天府旅游名宿——恩阳万寿村张家院子
右图　张学金 / 摄
恩阳万寿村“寿”景

Left Photo / Fu Haixu
Zhang's Courtyard in Wanshou Village, Sichuan Tourist Homestay
Right Photo / Zhang Xuejin
"Longevity" Scene in Wanshou Village, Enyang

Wanshou Healthcare Valley

This scenic spot, located in Bazhong's Wanshou Village, Xiabamiao Town, Enyang District, is a national AAAA-level tourist scenic area, Sichuan's Forest healthcare base, and its first batch of key rural tourism villages. Within its area of 28 million square meters, there are three spots such as Wanshou Lake Water Conservancy, Rose Cultural Industrial Park, and National Agricultural Sc-tech Park. The mountain and lake in it are beautiful, and the ancient houses elegant. There one sees the museum of village history, and exhibition hall of longevity culture, represented by turtle and crane in the Yishou Gallery, filled with profound longevity culture, blessing culture, folk culture, farming culture, and the same cultural heritage of food and medicine, hence a base for healthcare preservation, leisure and vacation, ecological tourism, and popular science education. The homestay of Zhang's Courtyard in the national forest village is one of Sichuan's famous tourist hotels, Wanshou is a forest village and beautiful leisure village at the national level.

1		
2	3	4

1　巴中日报社供图
恩阳空港花海景观
2　巴中日报社供图
恩阳海山村全景
3　付海旭 / 摄
恩阳海山村观光“小火车”
4　巴中日报社供图
恩阳空港会客厅

1. Photo / Courtesy of Bazhong Daily
Flowering Field, Enyang Airport
2. Photo / Courtesy of Bazhong Daily
Whole View of HaishanVillage, Enyang
3. Photo / Fu Haixu
Sightseeing Small Train in Haishan Village, Enyang
4. Photo / Courtesy of Bazhong Daily
Meeting Room, Enyang Airport

醉美玉湖·七彩长滩旅游景区

醉美玉湖·七彩长滩旅游景区位于南江县城西南部，面积 1.2 亿平方米，是国家 AAAA 级旅游景区、国家水利风景区、国家级森林康养试点建设基地。景区由玉湖、玉湖半岛、玉白渔村、黑池杨梅、花桥流水、七彩长滩、龙耳山等片区组成，有湖泊、山体、岛屿、森林、田园、古村落和红军文化、农耕文化、佛教文化、特色餐饮文化等文化旅游资源，集生态旅游、休闲度假、乡村旅游、水利科普等功能于一体。其中，七彩长滩景区有红枫园、盆景园、七彩槭树园等花木园区。

景区先后举办醉美玉湖龙舟赛、醉美玉湖桃花会、醉美玉湖庖汤节、醉美玉湖钓鱼抢鱼大赛、黑池杨梅采摘节、七彩长滩大酥肉节、七彩长滩彩林会等旅游节庆活动。景区所在的正直镇为四川省民间文化艺术之乡，长赤镇为省级生态乡镇、长赤镇青杠村为国家森林乡村，红光镇玉白村为全国生态文化村。

Zuimei Jade Lake · Colorful Long Beach

This scenic area, located in the southwest of Nanjiang, which covers 120 million square meters, is a national AAAA-level tourist and water conservancy one, and national pilot construction base for forest healthcare. It consists of Jade Lake, Jade Lake Peninsula, Yubai Fishing Village, Heichi Red Bayberry, Huaqiao Flowing Water, Colorful Long Beach, and Mt. Long'er, boasting lakes, mountains, islands, forests, pastoral fields, ancient villages, characteristic catering culture, Red Army culture, farming culture, Buddhist culture, and cultural tourism and integrating eco-tourism, leisure and vacation, rural tourism, and water conservancy. Among them, Colorful Long Beach includes gardens for red maple, bonsai and other flowers and trees.

Here such activities have been held as Zuimei Jade Lake Dragon Boat Race, Peach Blossom Festival, Soup Festival, Fishing Competition, Heichi Red Bayberry Picking Festival, Colorful Long Beach Big Crispy Meat Festival and Colored Forest Festival. Zhengzhi Town, site of the scenic spot, is home to Sichuan's folk culture and art, Changchi is a provincial-level ecological town, its Qinggang a national forest village, and Yubai, Hongguang Town, is a national ecological cultural village.

上图　玉湖长滩管理委员会供图
醉美玉湖景区
下图　南江县地方志办公室供图
南江长滩村七彩林业

Above Photo / Courtesy of Yuhu Long Beach Management Committee
Zuimei Jade Lake
Below Photo / Courtesy of Nanjiang Local Record Office
Colorful Forestry in Changtan Village, Nanjiang

1
2 3

1 程聪 / 摄
通江梨园坝村
2 张学金 / 摄
通江三李故居
3 通江县地方志办公室供图
通江方山旅游景区

1. Photo / Cheng Cong
Liyuanba Village, Tongjiang
2. Photo / Zhang Xuejin
Old Residence of Three Officials Surnamed Li
3. Photo / Courtesy of Tongjiang Local Records Office
Fangshan Scenic Spot, Tongjiang

中国传统村落——通江梨园坝村

梨园坝村位于通江县泥溪镇，为中国传统村落。该村现存穿斗木结构院落 58 套，其中明清建筑 28 套。有规模恢宏、雕刻精美的古墓 20 余座，其中南宋岩墓 3 座。后山有铁林城古寨，始建于明代，是米仓古道重要的军事基地。

Liyuanba, a Traditional Chinese Village

Liyuanba, located in Tongjiang's Nixi Town, is a traditional Chinese village. Of its 58 existing courtyards with tied-column wooden structures, 28 are of the Ming and Qing Dynasties. There are 20-odd ancient tombs of magnificent scale and exquisite carving, of which 3 of rock are in the Southern Song Dynasty. Behind it stays an ancient village named "Tielin City" (an important military base on Micang Ancient Road), which was built in the Ming Dynasty.

中国历史文化名镇——白衣镇

白衣镇位于平昌县东南部，是中国历史文化名镇、国家 AAAA 级旅游景区、国家级生态乡镇、四川最美古镇、四川特色文旅小镇。古镇历史文化悠久，为古柳州城遗址，现遗存有紫云宫大牌坊、观音大庙、节孝牌坊、吴氏宗祠、灵宫阁戏楼、钱庄、古井圈井、封火墙、岳飞手迹、魁星点斗等古迹。白衣全鱼宴是当地特色美食。白衣镇白衣庵社区为中国传统村落，白衣镇白衣庵社区、黄鹤社区为国家森林乡村。

平昌县文广旅局供图
平昌白衣古镇全景

Photo / Courtesy of Pingchang Bureau of Culture, Radio and Tourism
Whole View of Baiyi Ancient Town, Pingchang

Baiyi, Historical and Cultural Town in China

Baiyi, located in the southeast of Pingchang County, is one of China's historical and cultural towns, a national AAAA-level tourist scenic area, ecological town, one of Sichuan's most beautiful ancient towns, and characteristic cultural tourism town. This town, with a long history and culture and as the site of Ancient Liuzhou City, has now the large archway of Ziyun Palace, Guanyin Temple, Filial Piety Archway, Wu Family's Ancestral Hall, Linggong Pavilion Theater, Private Bank, Ancient Circle Well, Fire Wall, Yue Fei's Handwriting, Kwei Star Pointing to Big Dipper and so on. Baiyi All-Fish Feast is a local specialty here. Its Baiyi'an Community is a traditional Chinese village and, together with Huanghe Community of the same town, is one of the national forest villages.

1	2	
	3	
	4	5

1 匡亚 / 摄
平昌白衣古镇吴家大院
2 张学金 / 摄
平昌白衣古镇“魁”字景点
3 张学金 / 摄
平昌白衣古镇节孝牌坊
4 谢学程 / 摄
平昌白衣古镇古戏楼
5 卢文英 / 摄
平昌白衣古镇古封火墙

1. Photo / Kuang Ya
Wu Family's Courtyard in Baiyi Ancient Town, Pingchang
2. Photo / Zhang Xuejin
Character "Kui" in Baiyi Ancient Town, Pingchang
3. Photo / Zhang Xuejin
Archway of Filial Piety in Baiyi Ancient Town, Pingchang
4. Photo / Xie Xuecheng
Ancient Theater in Baiyi Ancient Town, Pingchang
5. Photo / Lu Wenying
Ancient Fire Wall of Baiyi Ancient Town, Pingchang

節孝

驷马水乡旅游景区

驷马水乡旅游景区位于平昌县驷马镇，是国家AAAA级旅游景区、四川十佳最美人工湖、国家湿地公园，是国家水利风景区江口水乡水利风景区、驷马河国家湿地公园的重要组成部分。驷马镇双城村是画家罗中立的油画《父亲》原型诞生地，有“《父亲》故里，山里水乡”之称。景区有巴山民宿、万家码头、水乡大峡谷、水乡大舞台、百里森林长廊等景点，并配套高空玻璃桥、悬崖秋千、高空溜索、滑草场、碰碰车、卡丁车、小火车等旅游项目，是湿地体验、度假养生、三产互动、观光农业、艺术写生、巴文化溯源、景民融合、新型工业等多业态综合性特色文化旅游地。景区所在地驷马镇为省级生态乡镇，驷马镇五峰村为国家森林乡村。

Sima Waterscape

This national AAAA-level tourist scenic area, located in Pingchang's Sima Town, is one of Sichuan's top ten most beautiful artificial lakes, national wetland park, and a key component of National Jiangkou Water Conservancy Scenic Area and Sima River Wetland Park. Shuangcheng Village of Sima Town is the birthplace for the oil painting of *Father* by painter Luo Zhongli. It includes Bashan Homestay, Wanjia Wharf, Grand Canyon, Grand Stage, Forest Corridor and so on, is equipped with such tourism items as high-altitude glass bridge, cliff swing, high-altitude zipline, grass skating field, bumper cars, go-karts, and small train are multi-format and comprehensive cultural tourism destinations such as wetland experience, vacation and health preservation, three-industry interaction, sightseeing agriculture, art sketching, traceability of Ba culture, integration of scenery and people, and new industries. Sima is itself a provincial ecological town, and its Wufeng is a national forest village.

1	
2	3

1 驷马水乡风景区管理委员会供图
平昌驷马水乡景区
2 张学金 / 摄
平昌驷马水乡水上乐园
3 付海旭 / 摄
平昌驷马大峡谷冲浪游乐

1. Photo / Courtesy of Sima Waterscape Management Committee
Sima Waterscape, Pingchang
2. Photo / Zhang Xuejin
Sima Waterscape Park, Pingchang
3. Photo / Fu Haixu
Sima Grand Canyon Surfing Amusement

上图　张学金 / 摄
油画《父亲》
下图　巴中日报社供图
平昌驷马镇双城村罗中立美术馆核心区

Top Photo / Zhang Xuejin
Father (Oil painting)
Bottom Photo / Courtesy of Bazhong Daily
Luo Zhongli Art Museum (Core Area), Shuangcheng Village, Sima Town, Pyeongchang

九寨山旅游景区
Mt. Jiuzhai

米仓山旅游景区
Mt. Micang

云顶茶乡旅游景区
Yunding Tea Farm

醉美玉湖 · 七彩长滩旅游景区
Zuimei Jade Lake·Colorful Long Beach

白衣古镇旅游景区
Baiyi Ancient Town

大石童话旅游景区
Dashi Fairy Tale

第三篇

康养

Part 3

Healthcare

巴中市花 / 杜鹃花（映山红）
City Flower/Azalea, Bazhong

第一章

康养基地

巴中是秦巴山片区三大中心城市之一，地处大巴山系米仓山南麓，位于中国秦岭—淮河南北分界线之南，有中国气候养生之都、国家森林城市、全国生态文明城市、全国最美生态宜居典范城市、四川省园林城市等美誉。巴中林地面积约 77.73 亿 平方米，森林覆盖率 63.18%，空气质量优良率达 95% 以上，负氧离子平均超过 10000 个 / 立方厘米，农产品优产率 85%，康养资源具有气候宜人、生态优美、康养福地、文旅胜地优势，是名副其实的生态绿肺、天然氧吧。

巴中森林资源丰富、生态环境优良、人文底蕴深厚，森林康养独具特色和魅力。全市有国家森林公园 4 个、国家森林康养基地 1 个、国家级森林康养试点建设基地 14 个、省级森林康养基地 28 个、省级森林康养人家 30 个、省级森林人家 11 个、市级森林康养基地 53 个、县（区）级森林康养精品点 102 个；有全国“绿水青山就是金山银山”实践创新基地 2 个、国家生态文明建设示范县 2 个、中国最佳养生休闲旅游名县 1 个、中国休闲度假养生养老福地 1 个、中国森林养生基地 1 个、中国森林体验基地 1 个、全国最美森林小镇 2 个。

丁伟 / 摄
光雾和谷国际森林康养小镇

Photo / Ding Wei
Town for Guangwuhegu International Forest Healthcare

Chapter 1

Healthcare Base

Bazhong, one of the three central cities in the Qinling-Bashan Mountains, is located at the southern foot of Mt. Micang, and in the south of the Qinling Mountains and the Huaihe River Boundary in China. It is known as the most beautiful ecological and livable city across the country and a garden city in Sichuan. The forest here is about 7.773 billion square meters with a coverage rate of 63.18%, air quality rate over 95%, average negative oxygen ion over 10,000 eachcubic centimeter, high yield of agricultural products up to 85%, and the resources here have such advantages as pleasant climate, ecological beauty, blessed land for healthcare and cultural tourism, which means a veritable ecological lung and natural oxygen bar.

Bazhong is rich in forest resources, excellent in ecological environment and profound in cultural heritage, which means a unique charm for healthcare. It boasts 4 national forest parks, 1 national forest healthcare base, 14 national forest healthcare pilot construction bases, 28 provincial forest healthcare bases, 30 provincial forest healthcare homes, and 11 provincial forest homes. There are 53 municipal-level forest healthcare bases, 102 county-or district-level forest healthcare points; 2 "clean waters and green mountains as invaluable assets" practice innovation bases, 2 ecological protection demonstration counties, 1 best county for healthcare, leisure tourism and elserly care, 1 place for leisure, vacation and healthcare, 1 forest healthcare base, 1 forest experience base, and 2 most beautiful forest towns, all at the national level.

张学金 / 摄
米仓晨雾

Photo / Zhang Xuejin
Morning Mist Around Mt. Micang

米仓山森林康养基地

米仓山森林康养基地位于巴中市文旅新区，是国家 AAAA 级旅游景区、国家森林公园、国家森林康养基地、全国森林康养基地试点单位、中华秦岭 100 景、四川森林康养国际合作示范基地、四川省最佳森林康养目的地、四川省首批国家级森林氧吧、四川省十佳国家级森林氧吧、群众喜爱的四川省十佳国家级森林氧吧。基地总面积 40155 万平方米，由牟阳故城、十八月潭、万字山风景游览区组成，年均气温 13 °C，有维管束植物 195 科、949 属、2597 种，野生动物 27 目、88 科、213 属、332 种。地文景观有山岳景观 3 个、山峰景观 6 个、峡谷景观 4 个、异洞景观 1 个、奇石景观 2 个、悬崖景观 11 个；水文景观有风景溪河景观 6 个、瀑布跌水景观 7 个、潭 3 个；生物景观有原始森林景观 3 个、动物景观 5 个；天象景观有 8 个；人文景观中主要有 3 个历史遗迹。

Mt. Micang Forest Healthcare Base

Located in the Bazhong Cultural Tourism New Area, this base is a AAAA-level tourist scenic area, forest park, forest healthcare base, pilot unit of forest healthcare base, and one of the 100 scenic spots in the Qinling Mountains, all at the national level, besides a demonstration base of forest healthcare for international cooperation. It is Sichuan's best forest healthcare destination, first batch of and top ten national forest oxygen bars popular with the masses. With a total area of 401.55 million square meters, it is composed of Mouyang Anncient City, Eighteen-Moon Pool, and Mt. Wanzi. Its average annual temperature is 13 °C. There are 195 families, 949 genera, 2597 species of vascular plants, and 27 orders, 88 families and 213 wild animals of 332 species. It boasts landscapes of 3 mountains, 6 peaks, 4 canyons, 1 unique cave, 2 strange rocks, and 11 cliffs; hydrological landscapes include 6 scenic rivers, 7 waterfalls and 3 pools; biological landscapes include 3 primitive forests and 5 animal scenic spots; and there are 8 astronomical landscapes and cultural landscape include 3 main historical relics.

光雾和谷国际森林康养小镇

光雾和谷国际森林康养小镇位于巴中市文旅新区光雾山镇。以光雾山森林资源和旅游资源为载体，以高品质养生服务体系为核心，配套有园林、医疗、体育、文化等公共基础设施，集聚山地运动、森林漫游、温泉养生、文化主题剧场等文旅项目，是既能游山玩水，又能休闲度假的特色旅游康养小镇。

大图　丁伟 / 摄
小图　巴中市林业局供图
光雾和谷国际森林康养木屋酒店

Big Photo / Ding Wei
Small Photo / Courtesy of Bazhong Forestry Bureau
Guangwuhegu Town for International Forest Healthcare

Guangwuhegu Town for International Forest Healthcare

Located in Bazhong's Guangwushan Town, Cultural Tourism New Area, this area, backed up by its local forest and tourism resources and high-quality healthcare service system, is equipped with public infrastructure such as gardens, medical care, sports, and culture, and gathers outdoor sports, forest walk, hot spring healthcare, and cultural theme theaters, which makes it an ideal place not only for lovers of mountains and rivers, but for vacationers.

天马山森林康养基地

天马山森林康养基地位于巴中市巴州区天马山镇，是国家森林公园、中国森林养生基地、四川省最佳森林康养目的地、四川省首批国家级森林氧吧、国家级森林康养试点建设基地。基地面积2297万平方米，包含天马山景区（有景点27个）和阴灵山景区（有景点22个）两部分，森林覆盖率为95%，是休憩、旅游、疗养、避暑胜地。基地主要景点有天马山、五马槽、酢房沟、蒿枝坪、古楼山、犟筋藤、鸳鸯树、南天门、四方碑等。

Mt. Tianma Forest Healthcare Base

Located in Bazhong's Tianmashan Town, Bazhou District, it is a national forest park plus healthcare base, one of the best forest healthcare destinations among the first national forest oxygen bars in Sichuan, and the national pilot construction base for forest healthcare. Its area of 22.97 million square meters with a forest coverage rate of 95% includes Mt. Tianma Scenic Area (with 27 scenic spots) and Mt. Yinling Scenic Area (with 22 scenic spots), hence a best place for tourism, leisure and summer escape. Its main spots are Tianmashan, Wumacao, Zuofanggou, Haozhiping, Guloushan, Jiangjinteng, Yuanyangshu, Nantianmen, and Sifangbei.

Photo (First from Left) / Courtesy of Bazhong Daily
House for Healthcare at Mt. Tianma
Photo (Second from Left) / Courtesy of Bazhong Daily
Holiday Inn at Mt. Tianma
Right Photo / Zhang Xuejin
Mt. Yinling

左一图　巴中日报社供图
天马山康养屋
左二图　巴中日报社供图
天马山度假酒店
右图　张学金 / 摄
阴灵山景区

巴中市史志馆供图
天马山林海

Photo / Courtesy of Bazhong History Museum
Sea of Forest at Mt. Tianma

中国美丽休闲乡村——西厢村

西厢村位于南江县赤溪镇，是中国美丽休闲乡村、国家森林乡村、天府旅游名村、四川省省级乡村旅游重点村。该村旅游资源丰富，有千年金丝楠木王、楠林古井、岳氏古牌坊、神窝石、丁字桥等旅游景观，有峡谷滑索、龙腾峡漂流、游乐场、卡丁车赛道等旅游项目，有稻田摸鱼、网红桥、竹筏亲水、萤火虫等观光体验区，有西厢记忆、留萤小筑、西厢水云间等巴山民宿，有村史馆、精忠文化产业园、青钱柳观光产业园、萤火虫养殖观赏基地等参观游览地。

Xixiang, China's Beautiful Leisure Village

Nanjiang's Xixiang, located in Chixi Town, is one of China's beautiful leisure villages, a forest village, and Sichuan's key and famous tourism village. Rich in tourism resources, it boasts the thousand-year-old Phoebe zhennan S. Lee, Ancient Well, Yue Family's Ancient Archway, Magical Nest Stone, and T-Shaped Bridge, in addition to canyon ziplines, Longteng Gorge rafting, playgrounds, and kart tracks. There are areas for sightseeing such as paddy field fishing, online-preferred bridge, and bamboo rafting, fireflies, besides homestay like memories of *The Romance of the West Chamber* and places like its museum of village history, Parks of Jingzhong Cultural Industry and Industrial Garden for Cyclocarya Paliurus, and Firefly Breeding and Watching Base.

1 张学金 / 摄
"留萤小筑" 巴山民宿
2 张学金 / 摄
千年金丝楠木
3 张学金 / 摄
"西厢记忆" 巴山民宿
4 张学金 / 摄
岳氏古牌坊

1. Photo / Zhang Xuejin
Liuying Xiaozhu Bashan Homestay
2. Photo / Zhang Xuejin
Thousand Year-Old Phoebe Zhennan S. Lee
3. Photo / Zhang Xuejin
Xixiang Village Named After *The Romance of the West Chamber*
4. Photo / Zhang Xuejin
Yue Family's Ancient Archway

1

2

3

4

大图　巴中市林业局供图
空山国家森林公园森林康养基地
小图　肖裕孟 / 摄
国家森林乡村——龙池新村

Big Photo / Courtesy of Bazhong Forestry Bureau
Forest Healthcare Base in Kongshan National Forest Park
Small Photo / Xiao Yumeng
New Longchi, National Forest Village

空山国家森林公园森林康养基地

空山国家森林公园森林康养基地位于巴中市文旅新区空山镇，是国家森林公园、全国森林康养基地试点建设单位、全国最美森林小镇、四川省森林康养基地、四川省首批国家级森林氧吧、四川省最佳森林康养目的地、四川 100 个最美观景拍摄点、四川最美林草景观。基地包括空山镇、两河口镇木诺槽村以及空山国有林场，有五大景区、56 个景点，被誉为“世外桃源、人间仙境、避暑胜地”。基地生物景观有维管束植物 329 科、2356 种，野生动物 67 种，地文景观 30 余个，水文景观 4 个，天象景观 2 个，人文景观 14 个。

Healthcare Base in Mt. Kongshan National Forest Park

This base, located in Kongshan Town, Bazhong's Cultural Tourism New Area, is a national forest park, national pilot unit for construction, most beautiful forest town, among the first forest oxygen bars and best forest healthcare destinations in Sichuan as well as its 100 most beautiful scenery shooting spots, and most beautiful forest and grass landscape. The base includes Kongshan Town, Munuocao Village of Lianghekou Town, and Kongshan State-Owned Forest Farm and 5 scenic areas of 56 spots, hence such titles as "Paradise, Fairyland, and Summer Resort". Its biological landscape includes 329 families and 2356 species of vascular plants, 67 species of wild animals, 30 geological, 4 hydrological, 2 astronomical, and 14 cultural sights.

唱歌石林森林康养基地

唱歌石林森林康养基地位于通江县唱歌镇，面积 14 平方千米，海拔 1200 米，是国家 AAAA 级旅游景区、全国森林康养基地试点单位、四川省森林康养基地。基地属川东北丹霞地貌，由一林（唱歌石林）二寺（牛石寺、门镇寺）三山（红花山、大钟山、双乳山）四寨（麻坝寨、龙池寨、鸡公寨、烟云寨）组成，有唐僧朝圣、一柱擎天、仙女思凡等景点 50 余个，奇形怪石 120 余个。基地所在地唱歌镇唱歌郎村石板溪为中国传统村落。

Changge Stone Forest Healthcare Base

Located in Tongjiang's Changge Town, this base, with an area of 14 square kilometers and 1,200 meters above sea level, is a national AAAA-level tourist scenic area and a national pilot one for forest healthcare. Of Danxia landform in northeastern Sichuan, it consists of one forest (Changge Stone Forest), two temples (Niushi and Menzhen), three mountains (Honghua, Dazhong and Shuangru) and four villages (Maba, Longchi, Jigong and Yanyun) with more than 50 famous scenic spots such as Tang Monk on a Pilgrimage, Heavenly Pillar, Fairy Down on Earth, besides 120-plus odd-shaped rocks. Shibanxi, where the scenic spot is located, is a traditional village of China.

唱歌石林研发中心供图
唱歌石林森林康养基地

Photo / Courtesy of Changge Stone Forest R&D Center
Changge Stone Forest Healthcare Base

上图　巴中日报社供图
唱歌石林景点
下图　肖裕孟 / 摄
中国传统村落——唱歌郎村石板溪

Above Photo / Courtesy of Bazhong Daily
Changge Stone Forest
Below Photo / Xiao Yumeng
Shibanxi, Traditional Village of China

镇龙山森林康养基地

镇龙山森林康养基地位于平昌县，是国家森林公园、四川省最佳森林康养目的地、四川省首批国家级森林氧吧、四川省森林康养基地。基地总面积 2553 万平方米，由镇龙山、佛头山、白衣古镇景区组成，年平均气温 12 °C，有维管束植物 120 科、319 属、498 种，野生动物 110 种。

Mt. Zhenlong Forest Healthcare Base

This base, located in Pingchang, is a national forest park, one of Sichuan's best forest healthcare destinations and first forest oxygen bars. With a total coverage of 25.53 million square meters and composed of Mt. Zhenlong, Mt. Fotou and Baiyi Ancient Town, it has an annual temperature is 12°C on average, possessing 498 species of vascular plants in 120 families, 319 genera and 110 species of wild animals.

巴中市林业局供图
镇龙山森林康养基地

Photo / Courtesy of Bazhong Forestry Bureau
Mt. Zhenlong Forest Healthcare Base

章怀山森林康养基地

章怀山森林康养基地位于巴中市恩阳区茶坝镇章怀村，是国家级森林康养试点建设基地，面积 1256.42 万平方米，森林覆盖率 58.66 %，空气中负氧离子含量最高为 2 万个 / 立方厘米。基地涵盖 72 座山、82 个洞、92 条山缝，风景秀丽，植被茂盛，有中药材百余种。基地主要景点有迎宾瀑布、九龙瀑布群、太子岩、太子洞、太子湖等，是集生态观光、游山乐水、寻古探幽、休闲度假康养、生态教研于一体的丘陵综合体景区。基地所在地章怀村为四川最美古村落。

Mt. Zhanghuai Forest Healthcare Base

This base is located in Bazhong's Zhanghuai Village, Chaba Town, Enyang District. It is a national pilot construction base for forest healthcare and covers an area of 12,564,200 square meters, with a forest coverage rate of 58.66% and a maximum content of 20,000 negative ions per cubic centimeter. With 72 mountains, 82 caves, and 92 crevices in the area, it enjoys beautiful scenery, lush vegetation, and 100-odd kinds of Chinese medicinal materials. With such main attractions as Yingbin Waterfall, Jiulong Waterfall Group, Prince Crag, Prince Cave and Prince Lake, it is a hilly complex scenic spot integrating ecological sightseeing, landscape sightseeing, exploration, leisure and recreation, and ecological education and research. The village, which contains the base, is among Sichuan's most beautiful ancient ones.

巴中市林业局供图
章怀山森林康养基地

Photo / Courtesy of Bazhong Forestry Bureau
Mt. Zhanghuai Healthcare Base

平昌县文广旅局供图
南天门森林康养基地

Photo / Courtesy of Pingchang Bureau of Culture, Radio and Tourism
Nantianmen Forest Healthcare Base

南天门森林康养基地

南天门森林康养基地位于平昌县五木镇，是国家 AAAA 级旅游景区、四川省森林康养基地，有四川 100 个最美景观之一“南天晴岚”拍摄点。基地面积 1850 万平方米，核心区面积 350 万平方米，系米仓古道重要节点、川陕苏区军事战略重地。基地主要由南天门森林运动公园、双河生态园组成，集红军文化、道教文化、民俗文化于一体。基地旅游景观资源丰富，有地文景观、水域景观、生物景观、天象与气候景观、遗址遗迹等 8 大类、15 亚类、27 种基本类型，有自驾游营地、太极广场、天池、瑶池、明山道院、樱花谷等，被誉为“生态田园画廊，运动养生天堂”。

Nantianmen Forest Healthcare Base

This base, located in Pingchang's Wumu Town, is a national AAAA-level tourist scenic area, Nantian Qinglan Shooting Site, one of Sichuan's 100 most beautiful landscapes. With an area of 18.5 million square meters, its core area being 3.5 million square meters, it was once the key node of Micang Ancient Road and military and strategic place of the Sichuan-Shaanxi Soviet Area. It is mainly composed of Nantianmen Forest Sports Park and Shuanghe Ecological Park, with Red Army culture, Taoist culture and folk culture integrated. In addition, its tourism landscape resources are so rich as to include 8 categories, 15 subcategories, and 27 basic types of cultural landscapes, waterscapes, biological landscapes, astronomical and climate landscapes, and relics. There are self-driving camps, Taiji Square, Tianchi and Yaochi Ponds, Mingshan Taoist Temple, Cherry Blossom Valley, etc., hence the name of "ecological pastoral gallery and paradise for sports and healthcare".

皇家山森林康养基地

皇家山森林康养基地位于平昌县西兴镇皇山村和土垭镇晨光村境内，面积 1260 万平方米，是国家 AAAA 级旅游景区、全国三十座最美茶园、国家级森林康养试点建设基地。基地内有长安古道、天子坟、犀牛望月、仙人下棋、神猴打鼓等自然景观，且巴人文化、长安古道文化交融。在两种文化基础上孕育诞生的翻山铰子为国家级非物质文化遗产，从而让皇家山森林康养基地成了集翻山铰子文化体验、茶旅康养于一体的康养旅游度假地。

平昌县委党史研究室供图
皇家山森林康养基地

Photo / Courtesy of Party History Research Office, Pingchang
Mt. Huangjia Forest Healthcare Base

Mt. Huangjia Forest Healthcare Base

Located within Huangshan and Chenguang Villages, Pingchang, with a coverage of 12.6 million square meters, it is a national AAAA-level tourist scenic area, one of China's 30 most beautiful tea gardens, and national pilot construction base for forest healthcare. It has natural landscapes such as Chang'an Ancient Road, Emperor's Tomb, Rhino Watching the Moon, Immortals at Chess, and Magical Monkey Hitting the Drum, and the local culture is blended with that of Chang'an Ancient Road. The dancing of Fanshanjiaozi, which was born of the two cultures, is a national intangible cultural heritage, thus making it a tourist resort integrated with cultural experience, tea tourism and healthcare.

桥亭森林康养基地

桥亭森林康养基地南江县桥亭镇，为省级森林康养基地。基地植被茂密，森林整体覆盖率 87%，年均气温 16.2 ℃左右，负氧离子含量约 2500 个 / 立方厘米。有物种 210 多种，其中珍稀树木达 20 余种，野生动物 50 余种。森林生态旅游产品丰富，打造森林康养漫步游、森林太极、森林瑜伽等森林康养运动，南江黄羊、药材、菌类等森林康养美食及青少年森林自然教育活动等。康养接待功能良好，设施齐全。

Qiaoting Forest Healthcare Base

As a provincial one of dense vegetation situated in Nanjiang's Qiaoting Town, it has a forest coverage rate of 87%, average annual temperature around 16.2°C, and content of negative oxygen ions about 2,500 per cubic centimeter. It possesses 210 species (including over 20 and 50 rare trees and wild animals, respectively), and is rich in forest eco-tourism products, including places for such sports as forest walk for healthcare, Tai Chi, yoga and others, in addition to delicacies like Nanjiang gazelles, medicinal materials and fungi, and forest nature education activities for youngsters. The healthcare reception here is excellent and facilities are complete.

张学金 / 摄
南江桥亭镇凤凰村

Photo / Zhang Xuejin
Fenghuang Village, Qiaoting Town, Nanjiang

第二章

康养产业

巴中森林康养产业具有得天独厚的“九度”（纬度、温度、湿度、高度、优产度、洁净度、绿化度、负氧度、精气度）优势，突出生态产业化、产业生态化，因地制宜，差异式错位发展森林康养全链业态，推进森林康养与巴人文化、红色文化、农耕文化、饮食文化、养生文化有机结合，形成集“吃、住、行、研、学、旅、体、赛、养”于一体的森林康养产业体系。既有南江黄羊、青峪黑猪、空山黄牛、山地梅花鸡等原生态牧业，通江银耳、大罗黄花、富硒茶、恩阳芦笋等生态有机农产品，全羊宴、全鱼宴、大酥肉、恩阳十大碗、农家腊肉、提糖麻饼、江口豆花青墉等美食，更有避暑、观景、徒步、滑雪、露营、探秘、摄影、写生等系列游乐项目。交通网络四通八达，航空、铁路、高速公路等交通出行便利。住宿设施设备齐全，既有费尔顿酒店等多家星级酒店，也有原汁原味巴山民宿，给游客宾至如归的享受。通过森林康养、营养膳食、修心养性、关爱环境等各种方式，让人在身体、心智和精神上都能达到自然和谐的优越状态。

巴中市文旅集团供图
贾郭山景点

Photo / Courtesy of Bazhong Cultural Tourism Group
Mt. Jiaguo

Chapter 1

Healthcare Industry

This industry has such 9 unique advantages as latitude, temperature, humidity, altitude, high yield, cleanness, greenness, negative oxygen, and freshness, highlighting the blending of industrialization and ecology, and following the local conditions, differentiated and staggered development of the whole chain of forest healthcare, promoting the organic integration of forest healthcare with the culture of Ba people, revolutionaries, farming, food, and health, hence a systemic industry of forest healthcare regarding "eating, living, traveling, research, learning, travel, sports, competition, and healthcare". At the same time, It boasts ecological animal husbandry (like Nanjiang gazelle, Qingyu black pig, Kongshan yellow cattle, and Shandimeihua chicken), ecological and organic agricultural products (Tongjiang tremella, Daluo daylily, selenium-enriched tea, and Enyang asparagus), delicacies (all-sheep and all-fish feasts, big crispy meat, Enyang ten bowls, home-made bacon, sugared sesame cake, and Jiangkou carp cooked with tofu) as well as recreational items such as summer vacation, sightseeing, hiking, skiing, camping, secret exploration, photography, and sketching. Such transportation networks here as air, railway and expressway are within each easy, in addition to well-equipped accommodation facilities like star-rated hotels such as Felton Hotel, authentic Bashan homestays, giving tourists a home away from home. Through forest healthcare, nutritious diet, self-cultivation, care for the environment and so on, one can achieve a natural and harmonious state in body, mind and spirit.

特色美食 Local Delicacies

1 巴中市文化馆供图
南江沙河鱼干饭
2 张学金 / 摄
恩阳芦笙养生汤
3 张学金 / 摄
巴中枣林船家子鱼
4 王建华 / 摄
平昌白衣全鱼宴
5 何嗣猛 / 摄
通江银耳汤
6 张学金 / 摄
恩阳提糖麻饼
7 张学金 / 摄
南江正直大酥肉
8 巴中市文化馆供图
平昌江口豆花青鳙
9 南江黄羊科学研究所供图
南江黄羊滋补汤锅
10 张学金 / 摄
恩阳古镇十大碗
11 张学金 / 摄
巴州魏油茶

1. Photo / Courtesy of Bazhong Cultural Center
Shahe Rice and Dried Fish, Nanjiang
2. Photo / Zhang Xuejin
Healthful Asparagus Soup, Enyang
3. Photo / Zhang Xuejin
Fish from Zaolin River, Bazhong
4. Photo / Wang Jianhua
Baiyi All-Fish Feast, Pingchang
5. Photo / He Yimeng
Tongjiang Tremella Soup
6. Photo / Zhang Xuejin
Enyang Sugared Sesame Cake
7. Photo / Zhang Xuejin
Zhengzhi Crispy Pork, Nanjiang
8. Photo / Courtesy of Bazhong Cultural Center
Jiangkou Green Bighead Carp with Tofu, Pingchang
9. Photo / Courtesy of Nanjiang Research Institute
Nourishing Soup Pot of Nanjiang Gazelle
10. Photo / Zhang Xuejin
Ten Dishes, Enyang Ancient Town
11. Photo / Zhang Xuejin
Bazhou Snacks of Weiyoucha

5

7

8

10

11

9

驰名酒业　Well-Known Liquor Industry

1	2
3	

1　辜天清供图
全丰酒原酒老窖池
2　杜晓华供图
小角楼酒生产线
3　李剑供图
江口醇酒百年池窖

1. Photo / Gu Tianqing
Ancient Cellar for Quanfeng Brut Baijiu
2. Photo / Du Xiaohua
Xiaojiaolou Liquor Production Line
3. Photo / Li Jian
Jiangkouchun Liquor Century Cellar

文创产品 Creative and Cultural Products

巴中市文旅商品相关企业（单位）供图
Photo / Courtesy of Cultural Tourism Commodity-Relevant Enterprises (Units), Bazhong

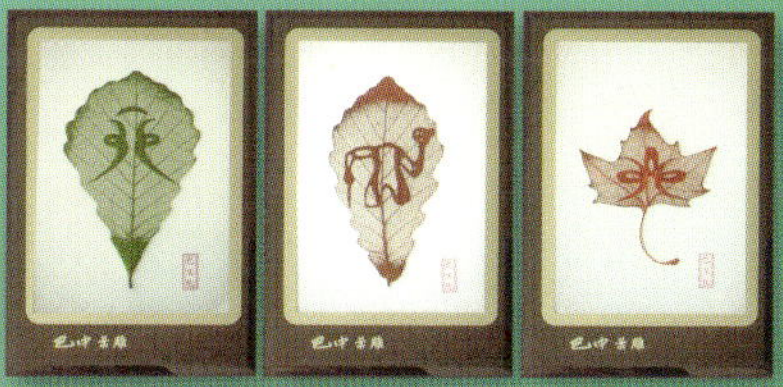

叶脉雕
Carving of leaf vein

叶脉画熊猫
Panda of leaf vein painting

平分土地
Equal distribution of land

巴山竹编工艺品
Bashan bamboo crafts

飞天扇
Flying fan

环保杯垫
Eco-friendly coaster

《时令巴中》
Bazhong's Seasonal Delicacies

通江银耳文创产品
Tongjiang tremella

翻山铰子·公道杯旅行套装
Dancing of Fanshanjianzi-Fairness Cup Travel Kit

太子攻书玩偶
Reading Prince (Doll)

川陕革命根据地博物馆文物邮票
Cultural Relics Stamps, Museum of Sichuan-Shaanxi Revolutionary Base

恩阳古镇丝巾
Silk Scarf in Enyang Ancient Town

星级宾馆　Starred Hotels

1　通江长盛大酒店供图
1. Photo / Courtesy of Tongjiang Changsheng Hotel
通江长盛大酒店
Tongjiang Changsheng Hotel
2　宋雪梅供图
2. Photo / Song Xuemei
南江桃园大酒店
Taoyuan Hotel, Tongjiang
3　王旭供图
3. Photo / Wang Xu
恩阳锦江饭店
Jinjang Hotel, Enyang
4　张学金 / 摄
4. Photo / Zhang Xuejin
巴中费尔顿大酒店
Felton Hotel, Bazhong
5　杨浩供图
5. Photo / Yang Hao
平昌龙熙国际大酒店
Longxi International Hotel, Pingchang

1

2

3

4

5

交通体系

Transportation System

1　邓林森 / 摄
巴城南环线燕飞互通立交桥
2　张学金 / 摄
全国首条红色高速镇（巴）广（安）高速王（坪）通（江）段
3　张学金 / 摄
恩阳机场
4　张学金 / 摄
成（都）巴（中）列车
5　卜寿林 / 摄
光雾山景区路

1

1. Photo / Deng Linsen
Yanfei Overpass, Bazhong Southern Ring Road
2. Photo / Zhang Xuejin
China's First Red-Themed Zhenba-Guang'an Expressway (Wangping-Tongjiang Section)
3. Photo / Zhang Xuejin
Enyang Airport
4. Photo / Zhang Xuejin
Chengdu-Bazhong Train
5. Photo / Bu Shoulin
Scenic Road in Mt. Guangwu

2

3

4

5

生态游乐 Ecological Amusement

左上图 夏雨 / 摄
第二十届四川光雾山国际红叶节
左下图 张学金 / 摄
四川 2022 恩阳龙舟公开赛
右上图 夏雨 / 摄
“梦境光雾山”山水夜游
右下图 夏雨 / 摄
“恩阳船说”夜游演出

Top Left Photo / Xia Yu
20th Sichuan Mt. Guangwu International Red Leaf Festival
Bottom Left Photo / Zhang Xuejin
Sichuan 2022 Enyang Dragon Boat Open
Top Right Photo / Xia Yu
Dreamland of Mt. Guangwu
Bottom Right Photo / Xia Yu
Night Tour of *The Legend of Enyang*

道地物产

Authentic Produce

1　南江县地方志办公室供图
南江长赤翡翠米
2　平昌县地方志办公室供图
皇家雀舌有机茶叶园
3　平昌县委党史研究室供图
平昌青花椒
4　肖裕孟 / 摄
通江中华老鹰茶树王
5　南江县地方志办公室供图
南江金银花
6　四川良源食品有限公司供图
南江核桃
7　中国通江银耳博物馆供图
通江银耳
8　李可 / 摄
恩阳芦笋
9　通江县地方志办公室供图
通江枳壳
10　张学金 / 摄
大罗黄花

1. Photo / Courtesy of Nanjiang Local Records Office
Changchi's Feicui Rice, Nanjiang
2. Photo / Courtesy of Pingchang Local Records Office
Queshe Organic Tea Garden, Huangjia Town
3. Photo / Courtesy of Party History Research Office, Pingchang
Pingchang Green Pepper
4. Photo / Xiao Yumeng
Chinese Eagle Tea Tree King, Tongjiang
5. Photo / Courtesy of Nanjiang Local Record Office
Nanjiang Honeysuckle
6. Photo / Courtesy of Liangyuan Food Co. Ltd., Sichuan
Nanjiang Walnut
7. Photo / Courtesy of China Tongjiang Tremella Museum
Tongjiang Tremellat
8. Photo / Li Ke
Enyang Asparagus
9. Photo / Courtesy of Tongjiang Local Records Office
Tongjiang Poncirus Trifoliata
10. Photo / Zhang Xuejin
Daluo Daylily

8

6

10

7

9

道地物产

Authentic Produce

左图　肖裕孟 / 摄
通江空山黄牛
右上图　李洪熙 / 摄
通江山地梅花鸡
右中图　南江县地方志办公室供图
南江黄羊
右下图　通江县地方志办公室供图
通江青峪黑猪

Left Photo / Xiao Yumeng
Kongshan Cattle, Tongjiang
Top Right Photo / Li Hongxi
Shandimeihua Chicken, Tongjiang
Middle Right Photo / Courtesy of Nanjiang Local Records Office
Nanjiang Gazelle
Bottom Right Photo / Courtesy of Tongjiang Local Records Office
Qingyu Black Pig, Tongjiang

乡村康养

1　通江县地方志办公室供图
通江沙溪镇王坪村
2　南江县地方志办公室供图
南江红光镇玉白村
3　巴中市巴州区史志研究中心供图
巴中市巴州区化成镇长潭河村
4　巴中经开区党政办供图
巴中经开区郑家山村
5　平昌县地方志办公室供图
平昌驷马镇创举村
6　巴中市恩阳区史志档案中心供图
巴中市恩阳区下八庙镇安居村

1. Photo / Courtesy of Tongjiang Local Records Office
Wangping Village, Shaxi Town, Tongjiang
2. Photo / Courtesy of Nanjiang Local Records Office
Yubai New Village, Hongguang Town, Nanjiang
3. Photo / Courtesy of Bazhou District History Research Center, Bazhong
Changtanhe Village, Huacheng Town, Bazhou District,Bazhong
4. Photo / Courtesy of Party and Government Office of Bazhong Economic Development Zone
Zhengjiashan Village, Bazhong Economic Development Zone
5. Photo / Courtesy of Pingchang Local Records Office
Chuangju Village, Sima Town, Pingchang
6. Photo / Courtesy of Enyang History Archives Center
Anju Village, Xiabamiao Town, Enyang District, Bazhong

参考文献

[1] 巴中市地方志编纂委员会 . 巴中市志 [M]. 北京：方志出版社，2014.10.

[2] 四川省巴中县志编纂委员会 . 巴中县志 [M]. 成都：巴蜀书社，1994.6.

[3] 四川省通江县志编纂委员会 . 通江县志 [M]. 成都：四川人民出版社，1998.8.

[4] 南江县志编委会 . 南江县志 [M]. 成都：成都出版社，1992.4.

[5] 四川省平昌县志编纂委员会 . 平昌县志 [M]. 成都：四川科学技术出版社，1990.3.

[6] 中共巴中市委党史办公室（巴中市地方志办公室）. 巴中市历史大事记（1993—2012）[M]. 北京：中共党史出版社，2013.12.

[7] 巴中市史志协会 . 巴中概览 [M]. 北京：中国文史出版社，2012.6.

[8] 巴中市地方志办公室 . 巴中年鉴 2014[M]. 北京：中国文史出版社，2014.12.

[9] 巴中市地方志办公室 . 巴中年鉴 2015[M]. 北京：中国文史出版社，2015.12.

[10] 巴中市地方志办公室 . 巴中年鉴 2016[M]. 北京：中国文史出版社，2017.3.

[11] 巴中市地方志办公室 . 巴中年鉴 2018[M]. 北京：中国文史出版社，2019.1.

[12] 巴中市地方志办公室 . 巴中年鉴 2019[M]. 成都：四川科学技术出版社，2020.9.

[13] 巴中市地方志办公室 . 巴中年鉴 2020[M]. 成都：成都地图出版社，2020.12.

[14] 巴中市地方志办公室 . 巴中年鉴 2021[M]. 成都：四川科学技术出版社，2021.11.

References

[1] Bazhong Local Records Compilation Committee. Bazhong Municipal Records [M]. Beijing: Publishing House of Local Records, 2014.10.

[2] Sichuan Bazhong County Records Compilation Committee. Bazhong County Records [M]. Chengdu: Bashu Book Club, 1994.6.

[3] Sichuan Tongjiang County Records Compilation Committee. Tongjiang County Records [M]. Chengdu: Sichuan People's Publishing House, 1998.8.

[4] Nanjiang County Records Editorial Committee. Nanjiang County Records [M]. Chengdu: Chengdu Press, 1992.4.

[5] Pingchang County Annals Compilation Committee, Sichuan Province. Pingchang County Records [M]. Chengdu: Sichuan Science and Technology Press, 1990.3.

[6] Party History Office of Bazhong Municipal Committee (Bazhong Local Records Office). Historical Events of Bazhong City (1993-2012) [M]. Beijing: Communist Party History Press, 2013.12.

[7] Bazhong History Association. Bazhong Overview [M]. Beijing: China Literature and History Publishing House, 2012.6.

[8] Bazhong Local Records Office. Bazhong Yearbook 2014 [M]. Beijing: China Literature and History Press, 2014.12.

[9] Bazhong Local Records Office. Bazhong Yearbook 2015 [M]. Beijing: China Literature and History Press, 2015.12.

[10] Bazhong Local Records Office. Bazhong Yearbook 2016 [M]. Beijing: China Literature and History Press, 2017.3.

[11] Bazhong Local Records Office. Bazhong Yearbook 2018 [M]. Beijing: China Literature and History Press, 2019.1.

[12] Bazhong Local Records Office. Bazhong Yearbook 2019 [M]. Chengdu: Sichuan Science and Technology Press, 2020.9.

[13] Bazhong Local Records Office. Bazhong Yearbook 2020 [M]. Chengdu: Chengdu Map Press, 2020.12.

[14] Bazhong Local Records Office. Bazhong Yearbook 2021 [M]. Chengdu: Sichuan Science and Technology Press, 2021.11.

附 录

重要文件

表 1

时间	单位	文件名
1994 年 2 月	中共巴中地委 巴中地区行政公署	关于加快发展旅游业的意见
1998 年 2 月	巴中地区行政公署	关于切实加强和改善文物工作的通知
1998 年 3 月	巴中地区行政公署	关于加快全区旅游业发展的决定
2005 年 4 月	中共巴中市委 巴中市人民政府	关于加强环境保护创建国家级生态示范市的意见
2005 年 6 月	中共巴中市委 巴中市人民政府	关于加快文化体制改革和文化产业发展的意见
2009 年 3 月	中共巴中市委 巴中市人民政府	关于加快文化建设的意见
2010 年 6 月	巴中市人民政府	关于加快旅游产业发展的意见
2012 年 1 月	中共巴中市委	关于加快建设文化强市的决定
2016 年 5 月	中共巴中市委 巴中市人民政府	关于大力发展森林康养产业的意见
2016 年 8 月	巴中市人民政府办公室	关于大力发展乡村旅游合作社的实施意见
2016 年 11 月	巴中市人民政府	巴中市森林康养产业发展总体规划（2016—2025 年）
2017 年 12 月	巴中市人民政府	巴中市促进旅游业发展扶持奖励措施
2018 年 2 月	四川省人民政府	关于《巴中市历史文化名城保护规划（2015—2030）》的批复
2018 年 5 月	中共巴中市委 巴中市人民政府	关于加快全域旅游发展的意见
2019 年 4 月	巴中市文化广播电视和旅游局	关于印发四川省巴中市全域旅游规划（2018—2035 年）的通知
2020 年 6 月	中共巴中市委 巴中市人民政府	关于加快文化和旅游融合发展的实施意见
2021 年 1 月	中共巴中市委办公室 巴中市人民政府办公室	巴中市促进文化旅游产业发展扶持奖励措施
2021 年 2 月	国务院	关于新时代支持革命老区振兴发展的意见
2021 年 10 月	四川省发展改革委	四川省“十四五”川陕革命老区发展规划
2021 年 10 月	四川省文化和旅游厅	四川省“十四五”文化和旅游发展规划
2021 年 11 月	国务院批复国家发展改革委	“十四五”特殊类型地区振兴发展规划
2021 年 11 月	中共巴中市委 巴中市人民政府	关于突破发展文旅康养首位产业的实施意见
2021 年 11 月	中共巴中市委办公室 巴中市人民政府办公室	巴中市文旅康养首位产业发展补充扶持措施
2022 年 7 月	巴中市人民政府	关于《巴中市“十四五”文化和旅游融合发展规划》的批复

Appendix

Key Documents

Table 1

Time	Unit	Document name
Feb, 1994	Bazhong Prefectural Party Committee Bazhong Prefectural Administrative Office	*Opinions on Accelerating the Development of Tourism*
Feb,1998	Bazhong Prefectural Administrative Office	*Notice on Effectively Strengthening and Improving the Work of Cultural Relics*
Mar, 1998	Bazhong Prefectural Administrative Office	*Decision on Accelerating the Development of Tourism in the Prefecture*
April, 2005	Bazhong Municipal Committee Bazhong Municipal People's Government	*Opinions on Strengthening Environmental Protection and Being a National Ecological Demonstration City*
Jun, 2005	Bazhong Municipal Committee Bazhong Municipal People's Government	*Opinions on Accelerating Cultural System Reform and Cultural Industry Development*
Mar,2009	Bazhong Municipal Committee Bazhong Municipal People's Government	*Opinions on Accelerating Cultural Construction*
Jun, 2010	Bazhong Municipal People's Government	*Opinions on Accelerating the Development of the Tourism Industry*
Jan, 2012	Bazhong Municipal Committee	*Decision on Accelerating the Construction of a Culturally Strong City*
May, 2016	Bazhong Municipal Committee Bazhong Municipal People's Government	*Opinions on Vigorous Development of the Forest Healthcare Industry*
Aug, 2016	Bazhong Municipal People's Government Office	*Implementation Opinions on Vigorously Developing Rural Tourism Cooperatives*
Nov, 2016	Bazhong Municipal People's Government	*Bazhong City Forest Health Industry Development Master Plan (2016-2025)*
Dec, 2017	Bazhong Municipal People's Government	*Bazhong's Support and Incentive Measures for Promoting Tourism Development*
Feb, 2018	Sichuan Provincial People's Government	*Approval of Bazhong Historical and Cultural City Protection Plan (2015-2030)*
May, 2018	Bazhong Municipal Committee Bazhong Municipal People's Government	*Opinions on Accelerating the Development of Global Tourism*

Continued table 1

April, 2019	Bazhong Municipal Bureau of Culture, Radio, Television and Tourism	*Notice on Printing and Distributing the Global Tourism Plan of Bazhong, Sichuan (2018-2035)*
Jun, 2020	Bazhong Municipal Committee Bazhong Municipal People's Government	*Implementation Opinions on Accelerating the Integrated Development of Culture and Tourism*
Jan, 2021	Bazhong Municipal Committee Office Bazhong Municipal People's Government	*Bazhong City's Support and Incentive Measures for Promoting the Development of Cultural Tourism Industry*
Feb, 2021	State Council	*Opinions on Supporting the Revitalization and Development of Old Revolutionary Areas in the New Era*
Oct, 2021	Sichuan Development and Reform Commission	*Fourteenth Five-Year Plan for the Development of the Old Revolutionary Areas in Sichuan and Shaanxi*
Oct, 2021	Sichuan Department of Culture and Tourism	*Sichuan's Fourteenth th Five-Year Plan for Cultural and Tourism Development*
Nov, 2021	State Council approves through National Development and Reform Commission	*Fourteenth Five-Year Plan for the Revitalization and Development of Special Types of Areas*
Nov, 2021	Bazhong Municipal Committee Bazhong Municipal People's Government	*Implementation Opinions on a Breakthrough Development of the Top-Priority Industry of Culture, Tourism and Healthcare*
Nov, 2021	Bazhong Municipal Committee Office Bazhong Municipal People's Government Office	*Supplementary Support Measures for Bazhong Development of Its Top-Priority Industry of Culture, Tourism and Healthcare*
Jul, 2022	Bazhong Municipal People's Government	*Approval of Bazhong's "14th Five-Year Plan" on Cultural and Tourism Integration Development Planning*

后记

我们守正创新、积极探索，以编纂出版《巴中文旅康养图志》（以下简称《图志》）的方式，全方位、多角度展现巴中深厚的文化底蕴、丰富的旅游资源、独特的康养优势，这既是落实全省文化和旅游发展大会，创新推动巴中文旅康养首位产业的具体举措，更是专业图志编纂的有益探索，借此希望给读者留下良好印象。

2022 年 3 月，中共巴中市委党史办公室（巴中市地方志办公室）正式成立《图志》编辑部，经过多次专题研究，拟定《图志》纲目，分别征求省地方志专家和全市各级各部门意见，力求框架设置既符合志书体例，又体现发展所需，并以中英文双语版呈现给广大读者。

在《图志》编纂过程中，坚持精益求精、优中选优，先后成立《图志》文稿编写组和图照采编组。文稿编写组从历年出版的市、县（区）志和综合年鉴，以及相关专业书籍中梳理和编辑文字资料，力求每章综合记述内容全面、特色突出、信息准确、语言精炼。图照采编组采取向摄影专家和市、县（区）相关部门征集，有偿购买服务等方式，共征集图照近 4000 幅，最终精选 330 余幅高质量图照放于成书之中。

本《图志》从筹划到实施，从文稿编写、图照征集、创意设计、具体制作到出版印制等各个环节，得到诸多方面的帮助和支持，特别是中国地方志指导小组、方志出版社、四川省地方志工作办公室的精心指导和倾情帮助，在此一并致谢！张学金、肖裕孟、王德平、谯杰、张光明等人也为本《图志》编纂出版提供了巨大支持！我们坚信，在相关组织、机构、专家和热心人士的努力下，本《图志》能够成为“诗意山水，红色巴中”的代表性名片。

由于编者学识有限，加之囿于时间仓促，对部分图照选取和文稿介绍尚有不足，敬请批评指正！再次感谢您在阅读中关注巴中文旅康养产业。

编者

2022 年 12 月

Postscript

We, while upholding fundamental principles and breaking new ground, have proactively compiled and published *Bazhong Pictorial Annals on Culture, Tourism and Healthcare* (Pictorial Annals, for short), showing its profound cultural heritage, colorful tourism resources, and unique healthcare industry in a fresh, all-round and multi-angle way. This is not only a specific measure to implement the provincial conference on cultural and tourism development, and innovatively promote the top-priority industry of Bazhong's culture, tourism and healthcare, but also a useful exploration of pictorial annals, by which readers may get a good impression.

In March 2022, the Party History Office (Local Records Office) under Bazhong Municipal Committee officially established the editorial department of "Pictorial Annals", which has ever since decided on its outline on the basis of repeated special study, opinions and suggestions from local record experts at the provincial and municipal levels, relevant leaders of the Municipal Party Committee and Government, and the authorities responsible, striving for a framework that follows the style of local records and meets the need for development. Besides, it has determined that a bilingual version (Chinese and English) be offered to the general readership.

While compiling, we have prioritized perfection and quality by means of two groups (for manuscript writing and photo editing): the former has sorted out and edited text materials from the annals and comprehensive yearbooks of the city and its counties (districts) published over the years, and related professional books as well, to achieve a comprehensive description of each chapter with comprehensive content, outstanding features, and accurate information, totaling a nearly 30,000-character manuscript, which is both brief and to the point; and the latter has edited or purchased nearly 4,000 photos from expert photographers and authorities concerned throughout the City, and finally selected 330 ones in the order of "quality first" to be used in this book.

From the planning to the implementation of the Pictorial Annals, and from the selection, design, production to the publication, we have received help and support from all sectors of society, so here we'd like to extend our special thanks to China Steering Group for Local Records, Publishing House of Local Records and Sichuan Work Office for Local Records for their untiring guidance and selfless assistance! We'd also like to offer our gratitude to such personages as Zhang Xuejin, Xiao Yumeng, Wang Deping, Qiao Jie, Zhang Guangming for their great help with the compiling and publishing of Pictorial Annals. We firmly believe that, with the concerted efforts of all the organizations, institutions, experts and enthusiasts concerned, this book will be a landmark for "Poetic Landscape and Heroic Bazhong".

Due to our limited knowledge and time, as far as the photo selection and manuscript wording are concerned, some deficiencies may exist. Therefore, we hope to hear your criticism and suggestions! Thanks again for your attention to Bazhong's culture, tourism and healthcare industry while reading.

Editorial Department

December 2022

剪纸《光雾山风景》 李亚雪作品
Paper-Cutting of Mt. Guangwu by Li Yaxue

中共巴中市委
巴中市人民政府 编

Compiled by Bazhong Municipal Party Committee and People's Government

内容简介
About the Content

发现美、传递美、感悟美，各美其美，美美与共。《巴中文旅康养图志》以简洁的语言、精美的图照、理性的阐释，让您领略美丽中国的巴中神韵。天赐自然美景与丰厚人文历史相得益彰，巴中之美，美在真实，美得醉人。与读者同行，与旅人共赏，巴中文旅康养留下的旅行记忆将是您永恒的乡愁，更美的巴中或许就在您的心中。翻开此书，巴中山水之奇、人文之盛、物产之丰渐次铺陈，扑面而来。

Beauty can be discovered, conveyed, felt and shared with each other. With its simple language, exquisite pictures (photos) and rational explanation, *Bazhong Pictorial Annals on Culture, Tourism and Healthcare* helps you appreciate the great charms of Bazhong, part of beautiful China. With natural scenery and cultural history complementing each other, Bazhong's beauty is both authentic and intoxicating. Whether you are a reader or tourist, we hope that memories of Bazhong and its beautiful landscape will stay fresh in your heart with you forever as a home away from home. Once you open this book, all wonders of Bazhong's mountains and rivers, together with its cultural richness and various products, will gradually unfold themselves before your very eyes.

读者服务 / Reader Service
4000213677 (028)87575393

协作团队
Collaborative Team

天下志鉴
A Local Records

四川天下志鉴文化传播有限公司是一家专业从事志书年鉴修编的机构，主要为政府机构和企事业单位提供编纂出版志书和年鉴的全流程服务。

Sichuan Tian Xia Zhi Jian Cultural Communication Co.,Ltd. provides professional whole process service of editing and publishing annals for government, enterprises and public institutions.Sichuan Tian Xia Zhi Jian Cultural Communication Co.,Ltd. provides professional whole process service of editing and publishing annals for government, enterprises and public institutions.

考拉看看
Koala Can

是由资深媒体人、作家、内容研究者和品牌运作者联合组建的内容机构，致力于领先的深度内容创作与运作，专业从事内容创作、内容挖掘、内容衍生品运作和品牌文化力打造。

A content institution jointly established by media experts, writers, content researchers and brand operators, committed to creation and operation of leading-edge and in-depth contents, specializing in content creation, content mining, content derivatives operation and cultural branding.

书服家
Forbooks

是一个专业的内容出版团队，致力于优质内容的发现和高品质出版，并通过多种出版形式，向更多人分享值得出版和分享的知识，以书和内容为媒，帮助更多人和机构发生联系。

A professional content publishing team committed to the discovery and publication of high-quality contents, sharing worthwhile ideas with people through multiple forms of publication, and thus acting as a bridge between people and institutions.

写作 | 研究 | 出版 | 推广 | IP 孵化
Writing Research Publishing Promotion IP incubation
电话 TEL 400-021-3677 Koalacan.com

图书在版编目（CIP）数据

巴中文旅康养图志 / 中共巴中市委，巴中市人民政府编 .—北京 ：方志出版社，2022.12（2024.12 重印）
ISBN 978-7-5144-5585-4

Ⅰ. ①巴… Ⅱ. ①中… ②巴… Ⅲ. ①旅游保健—旅游业发展—巴中—图集 Ⅳ. ①F592.771.4-64

中国版本图书馆 CIP 数据核字（2022）第 247753 号

责任编辑：程倩
责任校对：刘玉霞
责任印制：梅中英
出 版 者：方志出版社
地　　址：北京市朝阳区潘家园东里 9 号（国家方志馆 4 层）
邮　　编：100021
网　　址：http://www.zgfzcb.cn
发　　行：方志出版社图书营销中心（010-67110500）
印　　刷：四川科德彩色数码科技有限公司
开　　本：787 毫米 ×1092 毫米　1/16
印　　张：16.25
字　　数：402 千字
版　　次：2022 年 12 月第 1 版
印　　次：2024 年 12 月第 2 次印刷
定　　价：388.00 元